FORGIVING
THE UNFORGIVABLE

DAVID STOOP

Regal

From Gospel Light
Ventura, California, U.S.A.

PUBLISHED BY REGAL BOOKS
FROM GOSPEL LIGHT
VENTURA, CALIFORNIA, U.S.A.
PRINTED IN THE U.S.A.

Regal Books is a ministry of Gospel Light, a Christian publisher dedicated to serving the local church. We believe God's vision for Gospel Light is to provide church leaders with biblical, user-friendly materials that will help them evangelize, disciple and minister to children, youth and families.

It is our prayer that this Regal book will help you discover biblical truth for your own life and help you meet the needs of others. May God richly bless you.

For a free catalog of resources from Regal Books/Gospel Light, please call your Christian supplier or contact us at 1-800-4-GOSPEL or www.regalbooks.com.

To protect the privacy of some of the individuals whose stories are told in this book, names and characterizations have been fictionalized, although they are based on real events. With permission, real names and events are portrayed in most of the stories.

Servant Publications edition, titled *Real Solutions for Forgiving the Unforgivable*, published in 2001.

Servant Publications edition, titled *Forgiving the Unforgivable,* published in 2003.

Regal edition published in April 2005.

© 2001, 2003 David Stoop
All rights reserved.

Cover design by David Griffing

Library of Congress Cataloging-in-Publication Data

Stoop, David A.
 [Real solutions for forgiving the unforgivable]
 Forgiving the unforgivable / David Stoop.— Regal ed.
  p. cm.
 Originally published: Real solutions for forgiving the unforgivable. Ann Arbor, Mich. : Vine Books, c2001, in series: Real solutions series.
 Includes bibliographical references.
 ISBN 0-8307-3723-5 (trade pbk.)
 1. Forgiveness—Religious aspects—Christianity. I. Title.
BV4647.F55S76 2005
234'.5—dc22   2005000428

2   3   4   5   6   7   8   9   10   /   10   09   08   07   06

Rights for publishing this book in other languages are contracted by Gospel Light Worldwide, the international nonprofit ministry of Gospel Light. Gospel Light Worldwide also provides publishing and technical assistance to international publishers dedicated to producing Sunday School and Vacation Bible School curricula and books in the languages of the world. For additional information, visit www.gospellightworldwide.org; write to Gospel Light Worldwide, P.O. Box 3875, Ventura, CA 93006; or send an e-mail to info@gospellightworldwide.org.

PRAISE FOR

FORGIVING
THE UNFORGIVABLE

The Bible, as well as medical research, tells us that
forgiveness matters to your spiritual, emotional, relational and
physical health. But what does Christ-centered forgiveness look
like in the real world where many people see themselves as
victims and don't take responsibility for wrongs committed,
let alone ask for forgiveness? In this practical book,
Dave doesn't tiptoe around the tough questions. He faces head-
on the myths and misconceptions about forgiveness
and gives practical answers that can lead you to a deep
healing and a new sense of freedom. This is a book
you'll read more than once.

GARY J. OLIVER, TH.M., PH.D.
Executive Director, The Center for Marriage and Family Studies
at John Brown University
Coauthor, *Raising Sons and Loving It* and *Raising Kids to Love Jesus*

CONTENTS

Without forgiveness, there is no future.

BISHOP DESMOND TUTU

*If you forgive those who sin against you,
your heavenly Father will forgive you. But if you refuse
to forgive others, your Father will not
forgive your sins.*

JESUS OF NAZARETH (MATTHEW 6:14-15)

CHAPTER ONE

APOLOGY NOT ACCEPTED

The words she spoke of Mrs. Harris, lambs could not forgive . . . nor worms forget.

CHARLES DICKENS

Forgiveness doesn't come naturally to anyone. Perhaps the main reason is that it is so basically and totally unfair. I'm the one who has been injured, and now I must do the forgiving? No way! And if the offense is horrendous, forgiveness is not only unnatural, it seems impossible. Or what if the other person isn't sorry, or isn't even alive anymore. How do I forgive in that situation? It's impossible. Or is it?

A few years ago, I was confronted with some of the painful things I had experienced with my father as I was growing up. There was a sudden onslaught of memories of things I had tried to forget. Ever since my father had died, 20 years before, I had blocked out all the negatives of our relationship, trying only to remember the good things. But when the veil of my denial was broken by some remarks my sister made, I was flooded with memories of his Irish temper, of the vicious spankings in the basement, of my fear of him and of the ulcer I developed at age 10. Only then did I begin to reference that ulcer to the stress of living with his unpredictable temper. The myth had always been that my diet caused the ulcer—at least that was what I had always been told.

I knew I had to do something about all the feelings with which I was struggling. *But he's dead,* I remember thinking. *What am I supposed to do with all these horrible feelings?* I remembered what I told others in my counseling office, that forgiveness is the only way to resolve issues of the past. *But how can I forgive him when he's not here to be forgiven?* I asked myself. Yet a year later I was able to forgive him, and when I did, it was like my life had a new beginning. I understood the words of Pat Conroy, who wrote in one of his novels, "On the day I forgave my father, my life began."[1] What had seemed impossible became a reality.

But what if I had been called upon to forgive a more serious act, like murder? How do you forgive when your own child is murdered? And what if the one who commits the crime is also part of the family? How do you forgive someone you love for killing another loved one?

Wayne and Arlene attended our church. They had two beautiful daughters, both married and growing with their families. There was nothing apparent about the family that would make anyone think such a horrible thing could happen. Yet it happened. Wayne and Arlene's son-in-law shot and killed his wife, their daughter, during an argument in their kitchen. One can hardly imagine the pain Wayne and Arlene felt.

Then, in the midst of their grief, not only did Wayne and Arlene step in and take over the raising of their grandchildren, but they also stood by their son-in-law during his trial and prison term. When he was released, they invited him to live with them and his kids until he could get his life started again. The reality of the forgiveness given by Wayne and Arlene has been proved over the years by their actions.

But what if complete strangers killed your child? What if your beautiful young daughter was a Fulbright Scholar working halfway around the world, seeking to improve the lives of people trapped in poverty, and you suddenly were confronted with the reality of her brutal death?

Amy was a young woman from our community who was pouring her life into a black squatters' village in South Africa, helping the residents begin their slow march out of poverty after apartheid was eliminated. After spending over a year there, she felt the community was accepting her and her coworkers. Then the whole world heard the news that four young men from that same community had beaten her to death.

The world watched as her parents walked into the hearing room of the Truth and Reconciliation Commission and then publicly offered these men forgiveness, and stated that they would support the Truth and Reconciliation Commission if it decided to grant them amnesty—which it did. Yet it made the front page of our local paper only when Amy's parents talked about how they were going to help continue the work started by their daughter and set up a locally run business making "Amy's bread—the bread of hope and peace."[2]

What if the attack was on you personally? What if someone violated you and attempted to take your own life? Madge made news when she was assaulted and stabbed in a rape attempt. For 20 minutes she fought with her attacker in the ladies' restroom at a local restaurant. When he tried to escape, he was arrested in the parking lot. Madge was taken to the emergency room, covered with blood.

At the trial, months later, the man was sentenced to 17 years in prison. The judge then asked Madge if she wanted to make a statement. She made news again when she expressed to the court that she had forgiven the man and then said as she held up a *Living Bible*, "Your Honor, this man said that he knew he needed help, and I know that all the help he needs can be found in the Word of God." Since then she has visited and corresponded with her assailant, who has expressed remorse for his crime and amazement at having been forgiven.

How does someone forgive a betrayal? Judy tried to describe the pain she felt that horrible day five years ago. She said everything inside her was spinning and that she almost literally fell as she got out of her car. And then, as she was trying to steady herself, she heard a horrible moaning sound. Suddenly she realized the sound was coming from her. She said she felt the sound came from the depths of her soul and accurately marked the agony she was feeling. She had just found out that her husband had been into pornography since before their marriage 18 years earlier. She had also discovered that he had been involved in an affair for the past three years. Everything she had always believed about her marriage and family lay shattered at her feet.

Judy recalled how she and her husband had once joked about what would happen if either of them ever had an affair. She had told him, "It better never happen to us because I would be gone in a split second!" But now that it was a reality, her only thoughts were about how to find healing for such a huge wound within her soul, and how to salvage the marriage. Three years later, she had forgiven her husband, and together they had been working hard to create a whole new, healthy relationship as husband and wife.

What if you were the perpetrator? What if you were the one who did something unforgivable? How does forgiveness work when I'm the one needing forgiveness, and I feel like I can't forgive myself? It had been 15 years, but Irene couldn't talk about the abortions without breaking into convulsive sobs and then angrily berating herself for being so "wicked and stupid!" It didn't matter that her husband had been totally unsupportive as she felt so much pain over the years. It didn't matter that she had been struggling with her young daughter's potentially fatal illness, again without any support from her husband, when she had the two abortions. Nothing mattered to Irene except the horrible mistakes she had made years ago. It seemed impossible for her to forgive herself. Only when she started working at a local crisis pregnancy center, counseling young women faced with the same choice, was she able to work through her own forgiveness for the seemingly unforgivable actions she had taken in desperation years before.

WHAT IS UNFORGIVABLE?

Each of these stories is true, though some of the names have been changed, and each represents something unforgivable in some way. So when I was leading a workshop on forgiveness and the subject of unforgivable acts came up, I was ready.

"So what's unforgivable?" I asked the group as I moved toward the whiteboard. The first suggestions came quickly, and our list began to take shape:

- Child molestation
- Adultery
- Murder

"And especially if it's your child," someone added.

- Abortion
- Rape
- Divorce
- Abandonment by a parent
- Physical abuse by a parent or a spouse
- Any kind of betrayal by a loved one

Then suggestions started coming more slowly. People began suggesting things that were simply spin-offs, or specific examples, from what we had already listed. Or they were raising actions that were rather common but seemed more serious because of their circumstances.

Finally we agreed that the things on our list were the "heavies." They represented the major offenses that almost everyone was willing to place in the "unforgivable" category.

Then the discussion started to expand into larger events. Someone suggested the Holocaust as an unforgivable event in millions of people's lives. We talked about the horrible things done in South Africa in the name of apartheid. The atrocities done by both sides in Bosnia and Kosovo were recent enough for all to remember. That led someone to name the Arab-Israeli conflict, which is heating up even while I write this. And violence has been increasing again in Northern Ireland and other not-so-familiar places in the world. How do those who are touched directly by these events forgive? Are these acts unforgivable?

We next began to discuss the relative seriousness of the offenses we have experienced in our own lives. What may seem like a forgivable event to me may seem unforgivable to you. Some in the group said there were things in their lives that they didn't offer to put on the list because they were too personal and other people might not understand why these offenses felt unforgivable.

You may be thinking the same thing as you are reading this. What about my issue? What about that thing in my life that I consider to be unforgivable? As you read over the list above, you may think it is too general; it doesn't include some very specific offense that has taken place in your life. So we finally added to the bottom of the list the phrase "Other personal things too numerous to list specifically."

WHY IS SOMETHING UNFORGIVABLE?

What makes something feel like it is unforgivable? Is there a common element in those events? When people deal with personal issues, they typically see an unforgivable act as something done to us or to someone else that is (1) so out of the ordinary that it shakes our moral foundations to their roots—it goes against some very strongly held core belief—and, usually, (2) done by someone trusted and loved.

In each offense listed at the workshop, something was done that should not have been done, or something was not done that should have been done. In each instance a moral issue is raised. Even if the offender has died, he or she is on the list because of something done or not done. Murder, sexual abuse, adultery, abortion, rape, divorce, physical abuse, abandonment—each one is clearly a moral violation.

Forgiveness always involves the moral side of life. It involves our sense of right and wrong, of fairness, and of justice. It also involves our sense of love, compassion and mercy. When someone violates us with a seemingly unforgivable act, at least some of these values have been violated.

We then experience an internal conflict over how to resolve the conflict. For example, when someone we love betrays us, our values of right and wrong—or fairness—and of justice cry out for satisfaction. But we are torn, for there is another part of us that holds on to feelings of love for that person, compassion for their predicament, and a desire to show mercy. We are angry because of the tension between these two sets of values, which are competing for our attention. If we are to forgive, it feels like we must deny our own sense of justice and fairness. But *not* to forgive is to deny our sense of love and compassion. There is no easy way out of the predicament.

Even from a young age, we all have a sense of right and wrong and a concern for what is fair. Listen to a group of young children argue on a playground. Chances are, they will be arguing about something not being "fair." Or they may be arguing over their different interpretations of the rules.

We all have this early sense of what is bad and what is good behavior. Relationships are built on the foundation of our innate sense of morality. Without it we would experience chaos in our relationships and would probably avoid other people altogether.

When someone violates one of us in some hurtful way, not only is a moral principle being violated, but we also feel that something very important to us has been destroyed—our sense of innocence, for one thing. "How could this happen to *me?*" is the question that tears at the very core of our being. We had felt safe and protected, but now we feel exposed and vulnerable to the chaotic forces of evil. Our child has been taken from us. Our trust in the goodness of life has been shattered. The world is evil

Forgiveness always involves the moral side of life. It involves our sense of right and wrong, of fairness and of justice. It also involves our sense of love, compassion and mercy. When someone violates us with a seemingly unforgivable act, at least some of these values have been violated.

after all. In fact, there is no place that feels safe anymore—and no one who can be trusted. All of these thoughts and more now race through our minds and the thought of forgiveness becomes an unwelcome intrusion.

THE ALTERNATIVE TO FORGIVENESS—REVENGE!

Our natural desire for justice after unforgivable offenses often leads to thoughts of revenge, and those thoughts all too often feel good. Revenge has been called a wild but dangerous form of justice. But does it help? Revenge can often leave us with a haunting emptiness.

I was struck by the closing scenes of the movie *Dead Man Walking*. The parents of one of the murder victims were convinced that the murderer's execution would somehow release them from their pain and suffering. But the murderer's pain and suffering was in no way similar to their own, and retribution, no matter how just, did not provide any sense of satisfaction.

Revenge, no matter how just, can never bring satisfaction, for it can never replace what has been destroyed. It also brings us down to the level of the offender. There is an old saying that goes, "Doing an injury puts you below your enemy; revenging an injury makes you but even; forgiving it sets you above."[3] We usually do not even the score when we seek revenge; we merely set in motion a pattern of revenge. The lifelong feud between the Hatfields and the McCoys—and the Arab-Israeli conflict of today—shows us that revenge only leads to more injury. To get even only makes the other side feel he or she is now one down and so must retaliate in order to stay even. The offender becomes the offended, and on and on the cycle goes until all are destroyed.

When horrible things happen to us, there is typically a period of time when we fantasize all kinds of retributive punishment. However, staying with vengeful thoughts is like playing an endless and painful video in our minds over and over again. The desire for vengeance is always linked closely with hurtful memories of the event; we cannot separate the two.

An old Chinese proverb says, "He who seeks revenge should dig two graves," for not only does revenge harm the other person, but it destroys the one seeking it as well. The path that begins with revenge only leads downward to the grave. Not all anger is bad, but anger that is held onto eventually becomes bitterness, and anger and bitterness destroy us. They are killers.

One way the Bible describes anger and grudges is as a "root of bitterness." We are warned, "See to it that no one misses the grace of God and that no bitter root grows up to cause trouble and defile many" (Heb. 12:15, *NIV*). J. B. Phillips translates that verse this way: "Be careful that none of you fails to respond to the grace which God gives, for if he does there can very easily spring up in him a bitter spirit which is not only bad in itself but can also poison the lives of many others."

We've all seen examples of how a person's bitter spirit not only eventually destroys him or her, but it also hurts those who are around the bitter person. Why would anyone choose bitterness over forgiveness? It's easy to forget how good bitterness can feel. Proverbs tells us, "Each heart knows its own bitterness, and no one else can fully share its joy" (Prov. 14:10).

I've always found that proverb interesting for the way it couples bitterness with joy. The joy of bitterness almost sounds absurd, but no more absurd than our phrase "a pity party." While we may enjoy the fantasy of revenge for a season, we need to be very careful. Bitterness is very seductive and can easily draw us in, but the end of bitterness is always destruction.

FORGIVENESS DEFINED

If revenge—an eye for an eye and a tooth for a tooth—does not satisfy, what other choice do we have than forgiveness? There is no other way to deal effectively with the issues of the past. Confrontation often only leads to more hurt. Revenge is a dead end. We cannot redo our past, and once a wrong is done it cannot be undone. What other means do we have to resolve the issues that remain for us from past wrongs against us? How does God deal with the results of *our* wrongs? He does it through forgiveness. That is the only way we can deal with the hurts of our past. The premise of this book is that there is nothing that occurs in our lives that is beyond forgiveness.

Before we look at what keeps us from forgiving, let's define what we mean by forgiveness. David Augsburger notes, "To 'forgive' is, in the English language, an extended, expanded, strengthened form of the verb *to give*. By intensifying the verb we speak of giving at its deepest level, of self-giving, of giving *forth* and *giving up* deeply held parts of the self."[4] We *give up* the right to revenge, to perfection, to justice and instead we *give forth* to ourselves—or to the other person—freedom from the past and an openness toward the future. Forgiveness is a gift we give ourselves and others.

Webster provides several definitions of "forgiveness": "1. to grant pardon for or remission of (an offense, sin, etc.): absolve. 2. to cancel or remit (a debt, obligation, etc.): to forgive the interest owed on a loan. 3. to grant pardon to (a person). 4. to cease to feel resentment against: to forgive one's enemies. 5. to pardon an offense or an offender."[5]

Each of these definitions, especially the second, is in agreement with what the New Testament describes as forgiveness. In Colossians 2, Paul describes forgiveness. He writes, "You were dead because of your sins and because your sinful nature was not yet cut away. Then God made you alive with Christ. He forgave all our sins" (vv. 13-14). We might ask Paul here how God did that. The answer comes next. "He *canceled the record that contained the charges against us.* He took it and destroyed it by nailing it to Christ's cross" (v. 15, emphasis added).

To better understand what Paul is saying, think of a new Visa card that you received by mistake. It has a very high limit, and you can't resist the temptation. Within a week you have spent all it allows. You now have a debt you cannot possibly pay, even if the stores would take back what you bought.

Then, a couple of months later, someone from the Visa card company comes to your door. You haven't even been able to make the minimum payment, and you feel doomed. But you answer the door anyway. The company representative asks if you are the one who has made all these charges and then pulls out the "record that contained the charges against you." As you start to confess your foolishness in spending so much, and the mistake that was made in even using the card, the visitor interrupts you and says, "We know you made a mistake, but we came to tell you that someone else has paid off the card. Your 'debt has been canceled!' You don't owe us anything." In other words, you have been forgiven!

That would be pretty incredible, but that is exactly what God has done for us through the cross of Jesus Christ! He has taken the record of our sins, which produced a debt we could never pay, and he canceled it all. Our sins are forgiven!

Why, then, do some of us want to make certain things "unforgivable"? I think the only reason is that we have some wrong ideas about what forgiveness is and what it isn't. Let's check your "forgiveness" belief system.

QUESTIONS TO CONSIDER

1. How have you typically defined "forgiveness"?
2. What lessons did you learn in your family, while growing up, about forgiveness?
3. What things have you considered "unforgivable"?
4. What is the most difficult thing you have ever had to forgive?

CHAPTER TWO

MYTHS AND TRUTHS ABOUT FORGIVENESS

The stupid neither forgive nor forget; the naïve forgive and forget; the wise forgive but do not forget.

THOMAS SZASZ, M.D.

We each have our own unique set of beliefs about forgiveness. We have our qualifications about certain points, or our belief that some things are at least almost impossible to forgive. Let's examine our beliefs and understanding of forgiveness before we begin our examination of forgiving the unforgivable. Here's a short quiz that you can answer simply "true" or "false."

True False

T	F	1. When forgiving, I should always try to forgive and forget.
T	F	2. It's good to get angry when I'm trying to forgive.
T	F	3. I should give up all hard feelings toward the person I forgive.
T	F	4. I should try to forgive others quickly and completely.
T	F	5. Over time, my hurt will go away and my forgiveness of the other person will take care of itself.
T	F	6. If I've forgiven, I will never have feelings of hatred against those who have hurt me.
T	F	7. If I forgive, I am in some way saying that what happened to me didn't matter.
T	F	8. Forgiveness is basically a one-time decision. Either I forgive or I don't.
T	F	9. I can't forgive until the person who hurt me repents.
T	F	10. I should forgive even if the person who hurt me does not repent.

Let's look at each of the statements posed above as true-false questions and how we answered them.

STATEMENT 1:
When forgiving, I should always try to forgive and forget.

The answer is *false*, though if you answered true, you are not alone in that belief. I am amazed at how persistent it is. Whenever I speak on this subject, a number of people come up and say something about how they have always believed they were supposed to forgive and forget. I think part of the reason is that many of us were taught this at a young age and it stuck. How often did our mom say to us, "You just need to forgive that other child and forget about it"? And for many of the things that happened to us as children, it probably worked. It's also an adage that has been around for centuries. In fact, through literature, we can date it back in England to at least the fourteenth century.

Our belief that forgiving includes forgetting can be reinforced by our theology. We have been taught that when God forgives, he forgets. The promise in Jeremiah 31:34, repeated several times in Hebrews says, "I will forgive their wickedness and will never again remember their sins" (8:12; 10:17). In Psalm 103:12, David rejoices in the fact that God "has removed our rebellious acts as far away from us as the east is from the west." Obviously, God does forgive *and* forget. The question then is, "Don't I want to become more like God?" and if so, doesn't that mean I should eventually forgive as he does?

But how do spouses forget their partner's unfaithfulness? How does a parent forget about the child who was murdered? Or how does an adult forget about the abuse he or she experienced as a child? Try as we may, we can't forget. We may want to forget, but we really shouldn't forget.

Let me give you a simple example. Let's say that I'm speaking at your church for a weekend, and you like to talk to the guest speakers who visit your church. But you get very nervous thinking about it. Also imagine that you discovered one time by accident that if you stepped on the other person's foot and then apologized, your nervousness disappeared, so now you routinely step on the other person's foot, apologize, and then have a great conversation.

Now imagine that you have done this to me several times, and each time you have said you're sorry. And each time I have forgiven you. I'm a slow learner, but finally I catch on, so the next time you come up to talk to me, I say, "Stop. That's close enough!" You look hurt as you ask me, "What's wrong?" I tell you, "I know what's about to happen here. You're the one that always steps on my foot when we talk. Now my foot hurts, and I don't want you to do it again." You're shocked. You say to me, "But, Dave, I thought you forgave me for those earlier times." And I assure you, "I did, but I learned something about you, and I don't want you to step on my foot again. We can talk while you stand over there."

You see, I need to forgive *and remember*. The reason I need to remember is that you have a problem and I need to protect my foot. Why then can God forgive and forget? Basically because there is nothing he needs to learn in the process. He is omniscient—he knows everything. But I am not omniscient— I don't know everything—so I need to learn as I go along.

I vividly remember a young mother who came to see me. She was broken and very distraught, having just learned that her father had been molesting her eight-year-old daughter. As we talked, I sensed there was something more to the situation than she was telling me. I listened for a while and then asked her, "What else is going on in this situation?" She began to sob uncontrollably before she was finally able to say, "He did the same thing to me when I was that age."

After a few moments, I asked her to tell me how she had handled it in her own life. She told me that when she became pregnant with her daughter, she had seen a counselor about it, and eventually she had forgiven her father. Then, after a long pause, she added, "Not only did I forgive him, I worked very hard at forgetting what he had done to me. I didn't want to remember; it was too painful." I didn't need to say more. She realized exactly what she had just told me. She had tried to do the "godly thing"—to forgive and forget. However, she had also forgotten that her father had never acknowledged his wrongdoing. She had ignored the risk. He was dangerous, and he could and did do the same thing to her daughter. In remembering her hurt, she would have been able to protect her daughter. We need to forgive and remember, for when the hurt is deep, we need to learn something in the process about how to protect ourselves and those we love from having the same thing happen to them.

It is so painful to remember, however, that we don't like to do it. True, but when we experience real forgiveness, there is more to remember than the pain. We are reminded of what God has done and is doing in our lives through his forgiving us and our forgiving others!

STATEMENT 2:
It's good to get angry when I'm trying to forgive.

True. Not only is it OK to get angry as I work through the process of forgiving, it's a necessary part of the forgiving process. The deep hurts and injuries that seem impossible to forgive are neither quick nor easy to get over. We have a lot of emotion to process. We must grieve over what has been lost. For example, if I am dealing with forgiving a parent for abandoning me as a child, I am going to need to grieve over what I lost by that parent's absence in my life.

Each item on our "unforgivable" list represents something that has been lost. The molested child has lost his or her innocence, wholeness, and sense of safety and physical boundaries. An abortion is the loss of a life. Divorce results in the loss of an intact family and a relationship that was supposed to last a lifetime. And when someone we love betrays us, we lose trust, as well as the way we viewed that person before the betrayal. In fact, everything that calls for forgiveness on our part, whether we are forgiving ourselves or forgiving others, involves a loss of some kind, and we need to grieve over that loss.

Grieving begins with denial—believing this can't be true—and ends with acceptance of the reality that exists. In between these two stages of denial and acceptance are the two basic facets of grieving: anger and sadness. In order to process our grief, we must experience both anger and sadness, and in order to forgive, we must grieve. So anger is part of the process of forgiving.

What happens when we try to forgive without experiencing anger? Women, in particular, often have difficulty being angry. They feel sadness over their loss, but family and culture have trained them not to allow feelings of anger. Men typically have the opposite problem. They will feel anger over their loss but will not allow themselves to feel the sadness. In either case the result is the same: The individuals experience an incomplete process of grieving. They get stuck, and grief is unable to run its course.

STATEMENT 3:
I should give up all hard feelings toward the person I forgive.

Again, the answer here is *true*. This should have been an easy question to answer, especially if you looked back at the dictionary definition of "forgiveness." Webster said "forgiveness" means we "cease to feel resentment toward" the person who has hurt us.

The mark of forgiveness is that we no longer feel ill will toward the other person. We may not trust them anymore. We may not like them. But we don't wish them harm.

That doesn't mean there won't be times when those feelings come back. Often, after we have done the work of forgiving, something occurs in our life that seems to trigger all the old feelings of hurt and resentment. Does this mean we haven't forgiven? Not really. What it usually means is that we are working on the situation at a deeper level—a place deeper within us that needs to experience the healing of forgiving. We simply need to work through the forgiveness again at this new level of hurt. It does not negate what we have done before; it's just that there's more work that needs to be done.

STATEMENT 4:
I should try to forgive others quickly and completely.

Here the answer is *false*. True forgiveness is an internal process of healing that cannot be rushed.

Of course, it depends on the depth and seriousness of the offense. If you bump into me as we try go through a door at the same time and you say, "I'm sorry," I don't respond, "Well, I'll have to think about that. I'm not sure I can forgive you so quickly." That would be ridiculous. The offense was very small and easy to forgive quickly. In fact, when that happens, we usually don't say, "I'm sorry," we say, "Oh, excuse me."

But if you physically abused me and then only said, "I'm sorry," it would be equally ridiculous for me to forgive you quickly. Imagine that in a fit of rage you suddenly stab me with a knife. Then, as soon as you realize what you have done, you begin to apologize profusely, wanting, almost demanding that I forgive you. My response would probably include the idea that now isn't the time to talk about forgiveness. I need to get to a doctor quickly so that the wound can be dealt with and begin to heal. Talk to me in several weeks. Then we'll look at the issue of forgiving.

I had a young man call me for an emergency appointment. He was very distraught when he called, with good reason. He said he had just found out that his wife had been having an affair with his best friend. He had confronted her, and she had confessed and asked for forgiveness. He said they wanted the appointment because they wanted to save their marriage.

When they came in, I started by asking the young man how he was doing with the betrayal he had just experienced. He said, "I'm doing OK." I was surprised at his response, so I pressed him. I eventually pressed hard enough for him to become very irritated with me.

"Look, Doc, I'm a Christian. I've forgiven my wife," he responded forcefully.

His response was so strong that I went on to some other issues and then gave them an assignment to do together before the next session.

That weekend, he again called me in a panic. He was broken and in tears as he informed me that his wife had taken off again with his friend for the weekend. We talked a while, and then I said to him, "You know, we need to talk about your too-quick forgiveness. By trying to forgive your wife so quickly, you were basically saying to her 'no big deal.' And that's exactly how she heard it, as evidenced by her leaving again."

He agreed, so we talked about how, when someone hurts us deeply, we need to take some time to forgive. We make the decision early on that we will forgive, but we must take our time working through the forgiving process. It's neither quick nor easy.

I've found that our wanting to forgive quickly, even deep hurts, often comes down to a question of our wanting to forgive as God does. We read 1 John 1:9, "If we confess our sins to him, he is faithful and just to forgive us and to cleanse us from every wrong." When we ask ourselves, "How soon does God forgive us after we confess?" the answer is "Instantly!" And then, somehow, we believe that quickly is the Christian way to forgive.

However, that perspective is based on a small piece of the history of God's activities with us. We are looking only at the "post-cross" era. What if we lived, say, in 1000 B.C.—about the time David was establishing the city of Jerusalem? How soon did God forgive back then? It certainly wasn't instantly! And there was a tremendous price to pay. If we were living back then, when we sinned, we would have to offer either a sin offering or a guilt offering (see Lev. 4:1–6:7). But every time we sinned, we would have to repeat the sacrifice process because forgiveness was incomplete back then. Our sacrifices would have been mere "fore-shadows" of the true and final atonement, looking ahead to the cross and the perfect sacrifice of Christ that would complete our forgiveness (see Heb. 9:12-28).

Looking further back, to the Garden of Eden, we can begin to realize how God's delay had a distinct purpose. If God forgave instantly at that time, then all Adam and Eve would have needed to do was confess, and the problem would have been resolved. The opposite was true. They confessed, but their complete forgiveness was a long way off. God provided a temporary solution through the animals that were sacrificed, and he promised to resolve the problem in the right time, but the forgiveness was incomplete until Jesus said on the cross, "It is finished!"

So from Eden to the cross, God was in the process of forgiving. In Eden he made the decision to forgive, but the forgiveness wasn't complete until Christ was sacrificed on the cross. During the time between Eden and the cross, we encounter an emotion in God that is very disturbing to many, his wrath. Why is God so angry in the Old Testament, and why does he seem so different in the New? I believe he's the same God in both testaments. What we see in him in the Old Testament is part of his forgiving process. At times he even grieves over the fact that he has created humankind (see Gen. 6:6; Exod. 32:9). Because he is grieving, we see both anger and sadness in his character. Was God doing this because he needed to "work through his emotions"? I don't believe so. I think his anger filled another purpose, similar to one of the purposes of our anger in forgiving: *He wants us to understand how serious the offense of sin was and is.* He doesn't take sin lightly, and He doesn't want us to take sin lightly either.

Our taking our time to forgive, and our grieving over our loss through anger and sadness, helps us understand how serious the offense was. We don't want to take it lightly. In fact, forgiveness offered too quickly is not really forgiveness—it's excusing. And when we excuse hurtful behavior, we invite it to continue in our lives.

STATEMENT 5:
Over time, my hurt will go away and my forgiveness of the other person will take care of itself.

False. Forgiveness doesn't just happen. It always begins with a choice that leads us into the process of forgiveness. Failing to make this choice and simply waiting for time to heal the wounds is not forgiveness. Doing nothing merely represses our pain until a later time or another place. It has not gone away, it's just gone into hiding.

Although there is some truth in the statement, "Time heals all wounds," the healing referred to is not the same as forgiveness. Over time we may become desensitized to the pain, or we may repress much of our memory of the offense. Desensitization and repression are not forgiveness, however, and they do not provide the resolution and release from the past necessary for deep healing, which only comes through the process of forgiveness.

STATEMENT 6:
If I've forgiven, I will never have feelings of hatred against those who have hurt me.

The answer to this is *false*. When we have been deeply hurt, we may well have feelings of hatred toward the person who hurt us.

But, you may ask, isn't that counter to what Jesus tells us when he urges us to love even our enemies? I don't think so. Many think that hatred or anger is the opposite of love. This is far from true. The opposite of love is fear, not hate (see 1 John 4:18). In reality, it is hard to hate someone or something without experiencing some passion about it, and the passion comes from our loving or really caring about that someone or something. This person—or thing—*matters*.

While we may feel hatred toward the person who hurt us, we are not to stay in this negative emotion. Part of what we work through in forgiving is eventually letting go of these hurtful feelings. To do this, it is important to admit from the beginning, to ourselves and to someone else, that we have these intense feelings. Then, as we work on being able to forgive from our hearts, we are also working constructively on letting go of our hatred and anger.

STATEMENT 7:
If I forgive, I am in some way saying that what happened to me didn't matter.

False. Although it may seem as if we are condoning the hurtful act by forgiving, we are not condoning the evil. Forgiveness never makes an evil act into something good. In fact, the

*Forgiving other people does not in
any way benefit or let them off the hook.
It allows us to cancel the debt they owe us,
which in all probability they can never pay
anyway. We are the ones who are freed—
from the expectation of restitution for
the wrongs done to us.*

process of forgiving does quite the opposite. The depth of our sadness and anger is directly related to the seriousness of the injustice that has been done to us. Only by recognizing our pain, sadness and anger are we able to move forward in the forgiving process. God did not condone evil. He took it seriously enough to require payment for it—and then paid for it through Christ's death on the cross.

I think our concerns with condoning an evil act through forgiveness come from our inner sense of fairness and justice. It seems like we are letting the other person off too easily if we forgive them. Part of us cries out for the other person to pay somehow for what they did! We think that if we forgive our offenders, we are letting them off the hook.

While we may have these feelings, the truth of the matter is that forgiveness never has made sin OK. It has never turned an evil into something good. We can see this more clearly if we look at our relationship with God. Just because we have been forgiven by God doesn't mean we can go out and sin freely. Sin doesn't suddenly become OK.

Paul addresses this distortion in Romans 6:1-2, where he asks, "Well then, should we keep on sinning so that God can show us more and more kindness and forgiveness?" And he answers, "Of course not!" His response, "Of course not!" is the strongest you can make it in the Greek language—a triple negative. So if God's forgiveness doesn't condone sin, why would our forgiveness of a wrong done to us in some way condone the evil, hurtful event? It doesn't!

Although we protest that it would make it too easy for the perpetrator of our hurt, our forgiving the other person does not in any way benefit or let him or her off the hook. It allows us to cancel the debt they owe us, which in all probability they can never pay anyway. We are the ones who are freed—from the expectation of restitution for the wrongs done to us.

STATEMENT 8:
Forgiveness is basically a one-time decision. Either I forgive or I don't.

False. Or at least partly false. Forgiveness is both a decision and a process. Genuine forgiveness takes time. If God could take all the time between the Garden of Eden and the cross to complete the process of forgiving, what's our rush?

Every time I hear Arlene tell the story about how she and her husband decided so quickly to forgive their son-in-law after he murdered their daughter, I marvel. There was something truly miraculous in what they did. Much of the work of forgiving—the process of forgiving—probably took place after she and her husband made that decision. Judy took several years to work through her feelings before she was able to forgive her husband. And Irene took several months working in the Crisis Pregnancy Center before she was able to forgive herself. In each case, there was a decision that said, "Yes, I choose to forgive." Nevertheless, these people had to work through their grief, and that takes time.

One rule of thumb is, the earlier the injury took place in our lives, and the deeper the injury, the more time we typically need to work through the grief in the process of forgiveness. And we need a godly person to guide us during this time, for we don't want to get stuck in the bitterness or anger of the grieving process. We need an objective person we trust to walk with us through the grieving so he can tell us when the process is complete and it is time for the final decision of forgiving.

STATEMENT 9:
I can't forgive until the person who hurt me repents.

The answer is *false.* Perhaps you don't agree, so I'll briefly illustrate here and address the issue more fully in the next chapter.

A young man who had been admitted to the hospital for anxiety and depression shared his story in a group session. We were talking about forgiveness and the role of the offender in the process. He shared with us that a big part of why he was so anxious and depressed was that one of his pastors had hurt him deeply and refused to acknowledge that he had done so. I asked the young man why he didn't just forgive the pastor and go on with his life.

He protested rather strongly that in order for him to forgive, the pastor had to repent of what he had done. Without that repentance, the young man couldn't forgive. I said his reasoning seemed to put him in an impossible bind. We had been talking in group about how God required us to forgive. We had referred to Jesus' words in Matthew 6:14-15, "If you forgive those who sin against you, your heavenly Father will forgive you. But if you refuse to forgive others, your Father will not forgive your sins." We had talked about the fact that our forgiveness of others was an act of obedience to God.

This passage, and others like it, only served to make him more anxious, for he readily admitted that he wanted to be obedient and forgive, but he felt he couldn't. Finally I said to him, "I don't like your God." He looked at me, startled, and asked me why I would say such a thing. I said, "I don't like it that your God requires you to do something as an act of obedience, but then makes it impossible for you to do what he requires unless someone else cooperates." I went on to say, "The God I see in the Bible is one who requires certain things of me, but through his Holy Spirit, he makes it possible for me to do those things."

God requires us to be forgiving toward people. We both agreed on that point. But if the pastor never did admit that he had done wrong and repent of it, and that was a requirement for a person to be able to forgive, the young man was powerless to be obedient. He couldn't forgive. If I am required by God to be a forgiving person, then my ability to forgive must rest solely with me. It does not require the other person's participation.

STATEMENT 10:
I should forgive even if the person who hurt me does not repent.

This time the answer is *true*. The reasoning is the same as for the answer to the last question. But let me add, if my forgiveness is dependent on another person's willingness to repent, I am kept in the victim position and the other person holds all the power in the situation. Because forgiveness is not optional in the Christian's life, the choice to forgive must lie completely within me and not even partially in some other person. God can help me forgive without the cooperation of anyone else.

Basically, I am saying that forgiveness is an act done for the one who was hurt. The offender owes us, but he or she may never be able to repay even if he or she wants to. If we have to include them in the process, how could I have forgiven my father, who had been dead for over 20 years? Or how can we forgive someone who refuses to acknowledge the wrong he or she has done? Forgiveness offers release from carrying the burden of a debt that may never be repaid, even when it would be possible for the offender to make some form of restitution. Placing the power in the hands of the offender might work if he or she would acknowledge the wrong and repent, but if he or she refused, we would have been victimized not just once but twice.

QUESTIONS TO CONSIDER

1. For which of the 10 true/false statements were your answers different from those in this chapter?
2. With which of the chapter's answers do you still disagree? Why?
3. What new insights have you gained about forgiveness as a result of reading this chapter?
4. If forgiveness is not dependent on the perpetrator's repenting, how does that free us to forgive?

CHAPTER THREE

FORGIVENESS AND RECONCILIATION

*Forgiveness is no sweet, platonic ideal to be dispensed
to the world like perfume sprayed from a fragrance bottle.
It is achingly difficult.*

PHILIP YANCEY[1]

Whenever and wherever I speak on forgiveness, I am reminded that the main thing keeping people in a bind over forgiveness is the belief that forgiveness and reconciliation are one and the same. If I forgive, then I must be reconciled, regardless of what the other person says or does. Although it does not feel right, it may be what we've been taught.

It is important that we see forgiveness and reconciliation as two separate processes. Forgiveness is always necessary for there to be reconciliation, but forgiveness does not guarantee there will be reconciliation. My forgiving someone is not enough to ensure reconciliation—it also requires the genuine participation of the other person.

HOW MANY TIMES DO WE FORGIVE?

In Matthew 18, Jesus makes what may be his strongest statement about the nature of forgiveness. He has just finished talking about what we are to do when a brother sins against us, outlining the rules of confrontation and reconciliation. Then Peter asks a very practical question: "Lord, how many times shall I forgive my brother when he sins against me?" (v. 21, *NIV*). And then Peter adds very generously, "Up to seven times?"

To understand what Peter is saying here, we need to understand that the rabbis of his day commonly taught (and it is often still taught) that we only need to forgive someone who sins against us three times. After that we don't need to forgive, for the offender obviously was not sincere in their apology. Peter is being very generous when he suggests seven times. Why does Peter choose seven? Perhaps it is because seven represented the perfect number to first-century Jews. Or maybe Peter has been moved by Jesus' teaching and is in a very magnanimous mood. Whatever the reason, he is totally blown away by Jesus' response, "seventy times seven" (v. 22).

Some translations make it out to be seventy-seven times that we are to forgive. One ancient manuscript added the words "a day" to Jesus' response. Perhaps a monk copying that verse had had a particularly trying day. But in his addition to the manuscript, he really captured what Jesus is saying. Whether it is 77 times, 490 times or 490 times a day, Jesus is telling us that there is to be no limit to our forgiving.

THE UNFORGIVING SERVANT

To make the point more clearly, Jesus tells a parable about a king who was checking his books and found that a particular servant "owed him millions of dollars" (Matt. 18:24). When the man couldn't pay his debt, the king ordered that he, his whole family, and all his possessions be sold to pay the debt. (I always wondered how the man accumulated such an incredible debt when his net worth was probably only a couple of thousand dollars—but that's not the point of the parable.)

When the servant realized what was going to happen to him, Jesus said he "fell down before the king and begged him, 'Oh, sir, be patient with me, and I will pay it all'" (v. 26). At that, the king took pity on him and forgave his debt. There's the definition of forgiveness again—to cancel a debt.

I have tried to put myself in that man's place. I've imagined walking into my bank and hearing my banker say, "Dave, what about the money you owe us? When are you going to pay?" "Well," I reply, "just give me a little more time and I'll pay it. I still have some time left, don't I?" The banker thinks a moment and then says, "Oh, let's just cancel the loan—you don't owe us any money anymore!" Quite a fantasy! Not a bank in the world would do that. They only cancel the loans that are uncollec-table, and they only do that after agonizing over them and making every effort to collect what is owed them. But if they did do that for me, I would be walking on air as I went out the door.

That's not how the king's servant responded. He walked out of the king's office the same man as when he walked in; nothing inside of him had changed. He immediately met a friend—a fellow servant—who owed him a few hundred dollars. Jesus says the first servant grabbed his friend by the throat and demanded payment on the spot. Notice what happens next. Jesus says the friend "fell down before him and begged for a lit-tle more time. 'Be patient and I will pay it'" (v. 29). His behavior was identical to what the servant had just said and done to the king. You would think a lightbulb would go on in his head and he would think to himself something like, "Hey, that's what I just said to the king, and he forgave me my multimillion-dollar debt. Why am I hassling my friend for a couple of hundred bucks?" Instead, he did not show any sympathy toward his friend, nor did he show any understanding of the magnitude of what the king had just done for him in forgiving that huge debt. As a result, he had his friend put into prison until he could pay what he owed.

Fortunately, this second servant had some friends who knew the whole story and became so angered by what happened that they went and told the king about it. When the king heard what the first servant had done, he called for the man and said, "You evil servant! I forgave you that tremendous debt because you pleaded with me. Shouldn't you have mercy on your fellow servant, just as I had mercy on you?" (vv. 32-33). And with that, the king sent him to the same prison to which the servant had sent his friend, until the first servant could pay all of his multi-million-dollar debt.

WHO IS THE
UNFORGIVING SERVANT?

It's clear that I am the first servant in the parable and God is the king. The debt I owe is astronomical—I could never pay it if I lived 10 lifetimes. And the prison Jesus refers to is hell. The *New International Version* of the Bible says the king "turned him over to the jailers to be tortured, until he should pay back all he owed" (Matt. 18:34). The debt I owe is the result of my sin. Paul reminds us that the debt resulting from our sin can only be paid through our death (see Rom. 6:23). It is an unpayable debt: In order to pay it, I must die—a price I cannot afford. Only Christ can pay that debt for me through his death on the cross. Because of Christ, the king has canceled my debt. Through God's forgiveness, we can escape the penalty of sin and death and instead experience "the free gift of God [which] is eternal life through Christ Jesus our Lord."

Now we have a context by which we can understand the last thing Jesus says, which is the whole point of his teaching. Having presented the example of the unforgiving servant, Jesus says, "That's what my heavenly Father will do to you if you refuse to forgive your brothers and sisters in your heart" (Matt. 18:35). When I have been forgiven a debt I could never pay, I cannot *not* forgive. I don't have a choice anymore. I must forgive from the heart. Of course, as already pointed out, I need to take the time necessary for genuine forgiveness, I never condone the wrong by forgiving, and I will still remember. But I must forgive!

JOHN FROM LEBANON

I had the opportunity to teach for a week on forgiveness in an Addictive Behavior Counseling School in Amsterdam, Holland. The school is a part of the educational ministry of Youth With A Mission. It's always a privilege to teach in this school, partly because the students are an international group from all around the world.

During my free time one afternoon, a young man from Lebanon—we'll call him John—shared his story with me. When John was 20, a man in his village falsely charged John with a crime. The accuser lied and got several of his friends to lie. The law of the desert was that a matter is established by the word of two or three witnesses, and since no one could refute the lie, John was sentenced to 20 years in prison. As his accuser started to leave the court after sentencing, John looked at him and said, "I may be going to prison, but I have three brothers who aren't." The man heard him but hurried out of the court, having accomplished what he had set out to do. At the beginning of what had been expected to be the very best years of his life, John started serving his sentence.

There wasn't much to do in prison, so anything was a welcome diversion. A group of Bible college students came in once a week to hold services. John wasn't a believer, but he started attending the services, and soon gave his heart and life to the Lord Jesus. He then joined some of the other inmates in a small discipleship group led by the students during the week for those who had made commitments to the Lord.

It didn't take long for the issue of forgiveness to be raised as a part of obedience and discipleship. John was adamant. "I'll never forgive that man! How can I after what he's done to me?" Of course, the students pointed to the parable in Matthew 18 and to other passages in the New Testament where it is made very clear that forgiving is not an option for the believer.

It took a while for John to understand his need to forgive his accuser in the context of Jesus' forgiveness of him. Finally John could see the point. Although at first he was resistant, he began the process and knew that at some point in time he would need to forgive his accuser.

Then John answered the unasked question that was on my mind. He appeared to be in his early 30s, and he was not in prison. Obviously he had not served out his 20-year term. "In our country we do not get out of prison early for any reason. But at the five-year mark of my prison term, I was suddenly released," he explained. "To this day, I don't know why. I checked to make sure it wasn't some mistake, and then didn't check beyond that as I didn't want to make any waves."

After being released, John started attending the same Bible school that had sent the students to work in the prison. At the same time he continued to work through his understanding of forgiveness until he was able to "forgive from his heart" the man who had wronged him. As he continued to talk with students and faculty about what had happened to him, it seemed to him that God was telling him he needed to go to the man and tell him that he had forgiven him. When he brought this up to the students and faculty with whom he continued to meet, their reaction was quick. "Absolutely not, John. That man is dangerous, and you have no need to go and tell him!"

But God continued to lay it on his heart that he needed to go and tell the man. He finally convinced the others that this was from the Lord and that he needed to do this, so one Saturday morning a group of students and teachers gathered around John at the bus station and prayed for him before he boarded the bus to go back to his village.

When he got off the bus, no one in his village knew he had been released from prison. After his sentencing his family had moved away in disgrace. Now everyone thought John had somehow escaped and was here to exact revenge from the man who had wronged him. Excitement in the village increased as John headed for the man's house. When the man's wife finally answered his knock on the door, she informed John that her husband wasn't there. John simply replied, "Fine, I'll come back later."

Around suppertime John returned. This time, after John knocked several times, the man came to the door and cracked it open just a little. He was obviously quite nervous, not knowing why John was there.

"What do you want?" he asked.

"I came to tell you," John responded, "that while I was in prison, I met Jesus Christ as my Lord and Savior. I became a Christian. And as a part of my becoming a Christian, God forgave me for every wrong thing I had ever done in my life. And because I have been forgiven, I was able to forgive you."

There was a moment of silence as John's words started to sink in, and then the man threw the door open and said, "That's wonderful, John. Come and eat with us."

"No, thank you," John responded. "I really have no desire to eat with you. I just came to tell you that I've forgiven you." And with that, John turned and walked back to the bus station, got on the bus and headed back to school in Beirut.

As John and I talked, I was excited. He and his fellow students had gotten it right. Forgiveness must take place, but reconciliation is an option. John would have been foolish to have dinner with that man, who was dangerous and had already stolen five years from John's life. Who knows what lies he might have created if John had sat with him at dinner. We must forgive, but reconciliation is not always wise!

Forgiveness is a singular activity. It is something I do within me, and I don't need the other person to participate in the process for me to forgive. Reconciliation is a bilateral process, requiring the participation of both parties. For there to be genuine reconciliation, I need to forgive *and* the other person needs to show godly sorrow over what he or she has done. Forgiveness is required of us as believers, but reconciliation is optional and

For there to be genuine reconciliation,

I need to forgive, and the other person needs

to show godly sorrow over what he or she

has done. Forgiveness is required of us as

believers, but reconciliation is optional and

depends on the attitude of the offender.

depends on the attitude of the offender.

I wondered afterward about what might have happened if the man had responded differently to John. What would John have done if the man had said, "John, that's wonderful! I've become a believer also and that's why you're out of prison. When I became a believer, I wanted to make the wrongs in my life right and that meant I confessed that I had lied about you. Come and eat with us."

Would John have been required to eat with the man? I think if that had happened, John would have been wise to respond with something like, "That's great. And it's quite a surprise to me. I think I'll pass on dinner this time, but I'll get back to you." After leaving John could have checked out the man's story, and if it was true—who knows? Maybe he would have had dinner with the man and maybe not. Reconciliation, unlike the requirement to forgive, is an option.

JOSEPH FROM CANAAN

The same principle of separating forgiveness from reconciliation is also apparent in Joseph's experience. Genesis gives us a very honest picture of four generations in Abraham's family. We see them in all of their humanity, struggling with their marriages and with conflicts between their children—all the things we usually think only take place in our own families.

Genesis 37 provides a telling picture of the young Joseph. He was the spoiled child, the favorite of both Jacob and Rachel, which meant that Jacob did not show much favor to Joseph's 10 older brothers. On top of that, Joseph was a tattletale. He would come back to the house after helping tend his father's flocks and tell "his father some of the bad things his brothers were doing" (v. 2). That's pretty typical of the youngest child, but in Joseph's situation, it almost got him killed.

Several times, Scripture states that Joseph's brothers hated him and were jealous of him (see Gen. 37:4,8,11). To make matters worse, neither Joseph nor his parents seemed to be aware of the brothers' feelings toward him. Otherwise, why would Jacob have given Joseph the special robe, and then had him wear it as he went out to check on his brothers? Neither Jacob nor Joseph seemed to think twice about it (v. 13).

When Joseph's brothers saw him coming, they decided to kill him. Nice men, these brothers. But at least two of the brothers had cold feet. Reuben had a plan to rescue Joseph, and while Reuben was off trying to set up his plan, Judah proposed that they sell Joseph into slavery, saying "Let's not be responsible for his death; after all, he is our brother!" (v. 27). His suggestion carried the day, and Joseph was sold to Ishmaelite traders, who in turn sold him to Potiphar in Egypt. Potiphar was captain of the palace guard, a position that in Egypt included the duties of chief executioner—an interesting man to be your master!

But Joseph, for all of his naïveté within his family, was an accomplished administrator and had a genuine heart for God. Think of his circumstances—he was born free but was now a slave, and he was a Hebrew who now lived in a foreign land amidst a strange culture, including a language that was probably new to him. None of this was the result of anything he had consciously done. He was unaware of his brothers' animosity toward him. Up to the last, he had trusted them. And then, in Egypt, just when everything was going well, Potiphar's wife took an interest in him. Her lie of rape caused Potiphar to throw Joseph "into the prison where the king's prisoners were held" (Gen. 39:20). The unjust behavior of his brothers was now compounded by the lies of Potiphar's wife. And Joseph, who had enjoyed a degree of freedom even as a slave, was now imprisoned in this foreign land.

The time line suggests that his brothers sold Joseph into slavery when he was 17 years old. Perhaps he worked as Potiphar's slave for five years, since it might have taken him that long to rise to the position of being in charge of all of Potiphar's business and household. So he was probably about 23 when he was thrown into prison. Tradition says that Joseph was in prison for 13 years—until he was about 36. The years he spent locked up are typically considered the best of one's life.

His time in prison turned out to be part of Joseph's preparation for leadership. He had been a self-centered youth when he arrived in Egypt, and God had a lot of work to do to prepare Joseph for what his dreams had represented. During his confinement Joseph had to have come to terms with what had happened to him within his family. I imagine that he, like so many of us, would have described his family as "close." Perhaps he described his family to the other prisoners as they sat around during each day. When someone finally asked him "Who sold you into slavery?" Joseph would have answered, "My brothers." Then the next response would have been, "I thought your family was close." Gradually Joseph was faced with the reality of what he had experienced at the hands of his brothers.

Finally Joseph would have had to confront the truth and face the task of forgiveness. How else could he resolve the issues of his past? Forgiveness is the way God resolves the issues of our past, and it is the only way any of us can achieve such resolution. Now Joseph faced the same kind of decision faced by John, the young man from Lebanon. Joseph could hold on to the hurt and bitterness and destroy himself, or he could forgive. And, like John, he had to do so without any expectation of talking with, or even contacting, the persons he was forgiving.

I believe the evidence in Genesis shows clearly that Joseph forgave his brothers long before they appeared in his palace warehouse. So why did Joseph put his brothers through the trials we read about? I think he was testing the water, to see if they had changed and if it would be safe for him to reveal his identity to them—to reconcile with them. Some suggest he was getting revenge. I don't think so. He had become the second most powerful man in the world by then, and if he had wanted revenge, he could have done whatever he wanted with no questions asked.

Joseph tested his brothers to reveal the condition of their hearts. He did so by listening in on their conversation without their being aware of it. This was possible because he knew who they were but they had no idea who he was—or that he would be so familiar with their language. After all, he had been a 17-year-old Hebrew youth when they last saw him; now he simply appeared to be a middle-aged Egyptian.

The turning point came when Joseph demanded that they bring the youngest brother, Benjamin, to Egypt and then threatened to keep him in Egypt as his slave. Judah stepped forward to plead with Joseph. He told him about their father, Jacob, and his dedication to Benjamin, and about his pledge to Jacob to take care of Benjamin. And then Judah offered to be a substitute for Benjamin and to stay as Joseph's slave, partly because he could not "bear to see what this would do to him [my father]" (see Gen. 44:18-34).

This satisfied Joseph that God had changed his brothers' hearts, and he revealed himself to them (see Gen. 45:1-2). Later, after Jacob died, Joseph told his brothers that they didn't owe him anything, that he had forgiven them. The brothers were afraid, however, that Joseph would now exact revenge for their evil deed, so they sent a message to him, saying, "'Before your father died, he instructed us to say to you: "Forgive your brothers for the great evil they did to you." So we, the servants of the God of your father, beg you to forgive us.' When Joseph received the message, he broke down and wept" (Gen. 50:16-17). When the brothers came into Joseph's presence, Joseph again said to them, "Don't be afraid of me. Am I God, to judge and punish you? As far as I am concerned, God turned into good what you meant for evil" (vv. 19-20). Then Joseph assured them that he would take care of each of them and their families.

For Joseph to become the great leader he was in Egypt, he had to have broken the bondage of his great hurt and the woundedness he had experienced, from both his father's favoritism and his brothers' rejection and hatred. Only forgiveness can free the heart from the burdens of the past, releasing us to be what God wants us to be.

If reconciliation had been required for either John or Joseph to forgive, forgiveness would have been impossible. The work of forgiving was done by each individual without the involvement of the offending person. This was also true in Jesus' parable. The king did not ask his servant's permission to forgive him. In fact, the man never asked for forgiveness. In fact, he probably left the presence of the king fully intending to pay his debt, even after it had been forgiven. He continued to live as one who had never internalized the reality of his forgiveness. He refused to be reconciled to the truth of his forgiveness.

That's how God has forgiven us. He did not involve us in the process. He acted on his own. In the fullness of time, God sent his Son, Jesus, to die on the cross. The penalty of our sin was paid in full by someone else—by Jesus. He never asked, "Do you want me to pay the penalty for your sin?" He just did it. When Jesus died on the cross, the penalty for every sin that has ever been committed, and ever will be committed, was paid once and for all. The sin problem has been solved from God's side of the equation; God did it all by himself, without our involvement. He forgave us all our sins.

Does this mean everyone is forgiven? I believe so. Then why will some spend an eternity without God? It won't be because there is some sin that has not been forgiven. It will be because some people will have failed to be reconciled to the forgiving God. What is left now for each of us is to enter into the reconciliation process with the forgiving Savior. That begins with our showing godly sorrow over our sinfulness. That's the ongoing work of the church today. We are to proclaim the good news: We have all been forgiven! And the invitation is given to be reconciled to this forgiving God. Some hear the good news and say, "I don't need that. I've never done anything bad enough that I need forgiveness. Forget it!" Are they forgiven? I think so, although the point is moot for they refuse to be reconciled to the forgiving God. That's why the apostle Paul could say, "For God was in Christ, reconciling the world to himself, no longer counting people's sins against them. This is the wonderful message he has given us to tell others. We are Christ's ambassadors, and God is using us to speak to you. We urge you, as though Christ himself were here pleading with you, 'Be reconciled to God!'" (2 Cor. 5:19-20).

Paul then goes on and begs his reader "not to reject this marvelous message of God's great kindness" (2 Cor. 6:1). We have a choice. We can enter into the process with what God has already done on our behalf and be reconciled, or we can walk away like the servant in the parable—forgiven but unreconciled to the forgiving Savior.

Let's look now at why it is so hard for us to separate these two processes.

QUESTIONS TO CONSIDER

1. Why do you think we so often want to combine forgiveness and reconciliation?
2. What are some of the reasons why the forgiven servant in Matthew 18 couldn't internalize the reality of his own forgiveness so that he could forgive the debt of his friend?

3. What might have been some of the reasons why it would have been so hard for John to forgive the man who had lied about him?

4. If the work of forgiveness is completed, and the present work of the church is to proclaim the good news of that forgiveness, how does that change how we seek to evangelize others?

CHAPTER FOUR

A RADICAL
FORGIVENESS

To err is human, to forgive, divine.

ALEXANDER POPE

Many of us agree with Alexander Pope's statement that forgiveness is a divine action. Somehow we believe that God can forgive any way he wants, since he is God, but when it comes to humans forgiving, repentance is required. To many, Luke 17:3-4 teaches that we should not forgive except when the offender repents. Jesus says, "I am warning you! If another believer sins, rebuke him; then if he repents, forgive him. Even if he wrongs you seven times a day and each time turns again and asks forgiveness, forgive him." The idea that repentance and forgiveness go hand in hand is based on the words, "if he repents, forgive him," as if to say that we only forgive if he repents.

But look at the whole passage again, and in particular look at Jesus' statement about being wronged "seven times a day." Remember, the common teaching of that day was you only had to forgive someone three times. After that, the sin was on the other person for not changing their behavior. Jesus extended forgiveness beyond a "three times" total to seven times a day! Jesus calls us to a more radical type of forgiveness than was commonly taught in New Testament times. He is suggesting something more like, "When someone repents, how dare we *not* forgive." And we are also called to forgive even when someone doesn't repent!

FORGIVENESS IN THE OLD TESTAMENT

Several years ago my wife, Jan, and I were leading a weekend seminar on forgiveness at a church in Holland, Michigan. Following the seminar, a feature editor for the local newspaper, the *Holland Sentinel*, interviewed several of us on the nature of forgiveness.

One person interviewed was a Jewish law professor, who stated, "Forgiveness is appropriate only when the wrongdoer has repented. A woman is raped. Why should she have the burden of forgiving her rapist? She should only forgive when he repents."[1] He accurately represented Old Testament teaching. It is considered a *burden* for the person who is doing the forgiving (notice, he even used the word "burden"), and forgiveness is only required when the offender repents of his or her offense. This was and is the Jewish teaching on forgiveness. Islam teaches the same thing—forgiveness is required only in the context of repentance.

In fact, the Old Testament doesn't really deal directly with forgiving other people. There are three Hebrew words used for forgiveness, two of which are used only in relation to Divine forgiveness. The third word used in the Old Testament is primarily used in relation to God's forgiving, but it also refers to humans forgiving each other. Its use with human forgiveness is minimal—only three times. And each time, it teaches us nothing about human forgiveness. This word is used in Genesis 50:17, when Joseph's brothers implore Joseph to forgive them for what they had done to him; in Exodus 10:17, when Pharaoh asks both God and Moses to forgive him after the plague of locusts destroys everything in the land; and in 1 Samuel 25:28, when Abigail apologizes to King David as she intercedes for her wicked husband Nabal to keep David from killing him.

This Old Testament word literally means "to lift, to pardon, or to spare" someone. Joseph's brothers want him to "lift from them" the burden of their guilt. Pharaoh wants Moses to "lift from him" the foolishness of not listening to Moses. And Abigail wants David to "lift from her" the guilt, or foolishness, of her approaching him, the king. In each case, the one asking forgiveness is in a lower position than the one being asked to forgive; they are asking for something they do not deserve. In fact, in Old Testament times, forgiveness was seen as a sign of being weak. It was more of a virtue not to forgive. David's hatred of his enemies, as expressed in many of his psalms, is more the attitude of the typical Israelite.

In contrast, the other two Old Testament words for "forgiveness" deal only with God's forgiveness of humankind. God is always the subject of the verb; He is always the One doing the forgiving. This message of our forgiveness by God is unique to the Bible, as no other religious writing teaches that God forgives so completely and so graciously. In order for God to so graciously forgive us, two conditions must be met: (1) A life must be taken as a substitute for the sinner, and (2) The sinner must repent. This is distinctively Old Testament teaching, and is still true in regards to our becoming a child of God.

Given that historical context, it is easy to think Jesus was teaching that repentance and forgiveness must go together. With that mind-set, we could understand Luke 17 as confirming that view. I don't believe that was the intent of Jesus' teaching, however. He was focusing on forgiveness in the context of reconciling a relationship in which one has been called upon to rebuke sin and to help bring someone to a place of repentance. He is saying that when someone repents, we must forgive, even if that person hurts us over and over again. We go beyond forgiving three times and no more. That was a radical teaching in Jesus' day, and it still is. But the passage says nothing about what would happen if the other person refused to repent. Jesus is simply saying that whenever there is repentance, there must be forgiveness. This is part of the "good news" of the gospel.

THE SUNFLOWER

The Old Testament approach to forgiveness is the basis of the dilemma presented in the classic book *The Sunflower*, written by Holocaust survivor Simon Wiesenthal. In the book he described an incident that occurred when he was a young, Polish-Jewish prisoner in a Nazi extermination camp.

Prior to being imprisoned, Wiesenthal had watched as the Nazis forced his mother into a freight car jammed with other old Jewish women, after which he never saw her again. And he had watched the Nazis shoot his grandmother to death on the stairway of her home. Eventually 87 more of Wiesenthal's relatives would die during the horrors of the Holocaust, though Wiesenthal himself survived and later became the world's leading Nazi hunter.

One day in 1944, however, Wiesenthal and some of his fellow prisoners were assigned to carry rubbish out of a makeshift hospital for German casualties. While he was in the building—once a school that Wiesenthal had attended—a Red Cross nurse approached him and asked if he were a Jew. When he confirmed that he was, she signaled him to follow her and led him up a stairway and down a hall to a small, dark room where a lone soldier lay, heavily bandaged. The man's face was covered by white gauze, with openings cut out for his mouth, nose and ears. Then the nurse left Wiesenthal alone with the badly wounded soldier.

"My name is Karl," said a voice from within the bandages. "I must tell you of this horrible deed—tell you because you are a Jew."

Wiesenthal sat down on the edge of the bed and Karl began his story. He told of how he had been raised as a Catholic but lost his faith when he became part of the Hitler Youth Corps. He said he had served with distinction in the SS but had recently been seriously wounded on the Russian front.

Three times while Karl spoke, his voice reflecting his weakened state, Wiesenthal pulled away as if to leave. Each time the soldier reached out, grabbing him and begging him to stay. Finally he started talking about something that had happened while he was in Ukraine.

In the town of Dnipropetrovsk, booby traps left by the retreating Russian soldiers had killed 30 of the men in Karl's unit. In revenge, the Nazi soldiers had rounded up 300 Jews, herded them into a three-story house, doused it with gasoline, and fired grenades at it, setting the whole house ablaze. Karl and his men had surrounded the house, prepared to shoot anyone trying to escape.

"We heard screams and saw the flames eat their way from floor to floor," Karl continued. "We had our rifles ready to shoot down anyone who tried to escape from that blazing hell. . . . The screams from the house were horrible. Dense smoke poured out and choked us."[2]

At this point Wiesenthal loosened his hand from Karl's grip, but very quickly Karl grabbed it again and held on tightly.

"Please, please," he stammered, "don't go away. I have more to say. . . . Behind the windows of the second floor, I saw a man with a small child in his arms. His clothes were alight. By his side stood a woman, doubtless the mother of the child. With his free hand the man covered the child's eyes . . . then he jumped into the street.

"Seconds later the mother followed. Then from the other windows fell burning bodies. . . . We shot. . . . Oh, God!"

Finally Karl said, "I am left here with my guilt. In the last hours of my life you are with me. I do not know who you are, I only know that you are a Jew and that is enough." Karl sat up and put his hands together as if to pray. Then he said, "I want to die in peace, and so I need . . . I know that what I have told you is terrible. In the long nights while I have been waiting for death, time and time again I have longed to talk about it to a Jew and beg forgiveness from him."[3]

Wiesenthal described the thoughts that ran through his mind as he stood there in silence. "I looked through the window. The front of the building opposite was flooded in sunshine. The sun was high in the heavens. There was only a small triangular shadow in the courtyard. What a contrast between the glorious sunshine outside and the shadow of this bestial age here in the death chamber! Here lay a man in bed who wished to die in peace—but he could not because the memory of his terrible crime gave him no rest. And by him sat a man also doomed to die—but who did not want to die because he yearned to see the end of all the horror that blighted the world. . . . At last I made up my mind," he wrote, "and without a word I left the room."[4]

SHOULD HE HAVE FORGIVEN?

Obviously, Wiesenthal survived the Holocaust, but he was haunted by that experience. He wondered if he had done the right thing by walking out and not responding to the dying soldier. He asked his fellow prisoners, some of whom were devoted Jews who knew the Law and one who had been in training to be a priest. No one's answers satisfied him.

Some years later he wrote the story in detail. Then he asked 32 of the most religious and ethical men and women he could find "to mentally change places with me and ask yourself the crucial question, 'What would I have done?'"[5] Their responses are in the second half of the book. (In the book's second edition, the responses of an additional 21 are included.)

Of the 32 original respondents, only 6 said that Wiesenthal had been wrong in not offering forgiveness to the German. One contributor, novelist Cynthia Ozick, first commented on Wiesenthal's unconscious act of brushing a fly from the face of Karl as he spoke. She then summarized her remarks by saying, "Let the SS man die unshriven. Let him go to hell. Sooner the fly to God than he."[6]

Professor Alan L. Berger noted that Judaism teaches that there are two types of sins. One is committed by humans against God and the other is committed by humans against other humans. He said we can offer forgiveness to one who has sinned against us, but we cannot forgive one who has broken God's law and taken the life of another. The only one in that situation who has the right to forgive is the one who was murdered, and since he or she is dead, forgiveness is impossible.

Robert McAfee Brown, professor emeritus of Theology and Ethics at the Pacific School of Religion, described hearing a Holocaust survivor speaking at a memorial to those who had died. The speaker's theme was clear: *Never forget, never forgive.* He went on to talk about how we must never forget, and "that we must *never forgive* would seem to follow from the same stern logic"[7] as *never forget.* Brown struggled with the idea that forgiving could be a sign to persons in the future, causing them to think they could act without fear of punishment. He wrestled with the idea that forgiveness could be a "weak" virtue and thought of as condoning the evil. Like each of the contributors, he struggled with the enormity of Wiesenthal's predicament.

In the second edition of the book, radio talk-show host Dennis Prager wrestled with Wiesenthal's predicament and concluded his comments with a clear statement of the dichotomy between Jewish teaching and those of Jesus. For Prager it was clearly a moral wrong for a Jew to forgive a man who had burned families alive, but to the Christian it was equally obvious that one must forgive such a man. Prager understood the difference between the teachings of the Old Testament and the radical new teaching of Jesus.

JEWISH TEACHINGS ON FORGIVENESS

What can we learn from Wiesenthal's struggle? Perhaps the strongest message is to see how most of the world typically views forgiveness. Forgiveness is unfair; it is unjust; it defies human logic and reason—unless the offender repents and asks for forgiveness. Forgiveness must be conditional. It requires repentance, and there are therefore some things that are unforgivable.

This Jewish teaching is summed up by the Ramba'm in Hillel; Teshuvah 2:9-10, where he writes:

> Repentance and Yom Kippur only atone for sins between Man and God such as eating forbidden foods or engaging in forbidden sexual relations. Sins between one man and his fellow, such as striking, cursing, or stealing are never forgiven until one pays up his debt and appeases his fellow. Even if he returns the money he owes he must still ask for forgiveness. Even if he only spoke badly about him, he must appease and beseech until he is forgiven. If his fellow refuses to forgive him, he must then bring a group of three of his friends (presumably the injured party's friends) and go to him and ask him (for forgiveness). If he still does not forgive him he must go to him a second and third time (with a different group of three people). If he still refuses to forgive him he may cease and the other is the sinner. If (the injured party) is his teacher (rebbe) he must go to him even a thousand times until he is forgiven.

A person who does not forgive when asked is considered a cruel person. But he must be asked to do so before he can forgive. This is conditional forgiveness.

CHRISTIANS' CONDITIONAL FORGIVENESS

The concept of conditional forgiveness is not limited to Jews. Too many Christians still see it in the same light. Pick up any book on forgiveness—or on hurt and anger—and you will be all too likely to find that the offender's repentance is a required part of the resolution process. For example, a booklet published by the Radio Bible Class, *When Forgiveness Seems Impossible*, states,

> Forgiveness is one of the most misunderstood doctrines of the Christian life. Many believe that forgiveness requires us to unconditionally release others from past wrongs. They assume that we have to forgive in order to love. Others have adopted the "I forgive you for my own sake" attitude that advocates forgiveness as a means of releasing ourselves from the cancer of bitterness and the fire of anger. In many different ways, forgiveness is therefore seen as an unconditional offering of pardon that says, "No matter what you have done to me, I forgive you."[8]

I'm not sure why the author of this booklet is so opposed to the idea, "I forgive you for my own sake," since he or she admits that forgiveness releases us from the sins of bitterness and anger. However, we do get some insight into the author's reasoning from an example given to show when unconditional forgiveness could be harmful.

One shudders to think of a wife offering forgiveness to an unrepentant alcoholic husband who has privately beaten her and publicly humiliated her with his sexual affairs. Is such forgiveness the kind of love her husband needs? Is it in his best interest for her to release him from accountability for vicious violations of their marital vows?

The author assumes the answer would be "no," but why does he or she equate unconditional forgiveness with being a passive victim?

In a summary paragraph, the booklet says,

Sometimes love requires us to say, "Father, forgive them, for they do not know what they do" (Luke 23:34). Sometimes love requires us to forgive over and over (see Matt. 18:21-22). And sometimes love requires us to withhold forgiveness for the sake of the one who has harmed us.[9]

The author, however, provides no Scripture to support that last statement. In fact, no Scripture in the New Testament supports that Old Testament concept.

Much of what the booklet says is good, but in the process of forgiveness indicated, the step of repentance is right in the middle, preceded by the step of confrontation. It sounds just like the Mishnah, a centuries-old compilation of rabbinical commentaries on the Pentateuch. One must confront the wrongdoer, and if the wrongdoer repents, then one is to forgive. But if the wrongdoer doesn't repent, don't forgive.

But what are we to do if there is no repentance? Do we withhold forgiveness? And if we do that, how can we be obedient, forgiving followers of Jesus Christ?

Indeed, once confrontation and the offender's repentance are included as necessary parts of the process, forgiveness does become a burden. Jesus, on the other hand, took a much more radical—and freeing—approach, teaching that forgiveness is a *gift* of grace.

A RADICAL FORGIVENESS

What Jesus calls us to in Matthew 6 and Matthew 18 goes way beyond the Old Testament teachings. There is to be no limit to the number of times we forgive. We are to forgive and not keep count of how many times we forgive. We are to forgive even in the absence of repentance, for forgiveness is now unconditional. We are to forgive our enemies, even while they are still our

Once confrontation and the offender's repentance are included as necessary parts of the process, forgiveness does become a burden. Jesus, on the other hand, took a much more radical—and freeing—approach, teaching that forgiveness is a gift of grace.

enemies. And why are we to forgive like this? We are to forgive according to how much we have been forgiven by our loving heavenly Father.

The apostle Paul understood this concept well. In Romans 5, he uses three phrases to describe us—"utterly helpless", "sinners," and God's "enemies." He writes,

> When we were utterly helpless, Christ came at just the right time and died for us sinners. Now, no one is likely to die for a good person, though someone might be willing to die for a person who is especially good. But God showed his great love for us by sending Christ to die for us while we still sinners. And since we have been made right in God's sight by the blood of Christ, he will certainly save us from God's judgment. For since we were restored to friendship with God by the death of his Son while we were still his enemies, we will certainly be delivered from eternal punishment by his life. So now we can rejoice in our wonderful new relationship with God—all because of what our Lord Jesus Christ has done for us in making us friends of God (Rom. 5:6-11).

That's the nature of God's love and forgiveness for us while we were still his enemies. That's when he forgave us the debt we could never pay. Jesus paid it all so we could experience His incredible, unconditional forgiveness. All that's required of us is our response and willingness to receive His forgiveness. And out of the reality of that forgiveness, we become "forgiving people"!

Consider the story of Corrie ten Boom, who, like Wiesenthal, was imprisoned in one of the Nazi extermination camps during World War II. One day, after the war was over, she preached in Munich on the topic of forgiveness. After the service she came face-to-face with a man who had been one of her guards in the camp. For a moment she froze, flooded with horrible memories of that place. She said she had to pray, "Lord, forgive me, I cannot forgive," but as she prayed, the hatred melted away and she was able to shake his hand and experience forgiveness.

Or consider the story of Martin Luther King, Jr. While he was in the Birmingham city jail, mobs were outside yelling for his death and policemen attacked his unarmed supporters. With all this going on, he wrote that he had decided to fast for several days as an act of spiritual discipline, in order to be able to forgive those who were still calling for his death.

Or what about the act of Pope John Paul II? He descended into the depths of Rome's Rebibbia prison to visit Mehmet Ali Agca, the man who had tried to assassinate him during an event in St. Peter's Square—and nearly succeeded. The pope said three simple words, "I forgive you." The world was astonished by his act, so much so that *Time* magazine devoted a cover story to what they considered "a remarkable event." It was an act of unconditional forgiveness.

Or what about Nelson Mandela, who was imprisoned for 27 years because of his opposition to apartheid? While in prison he was forced to work in a stone quarry, where his eyesight was severely damaged by the intense light, and throughout those years, the state security police harassed his family. But when he was finally released from prison and became the first democratically elected president of South Africa, he invited his white jailer to attend the inauguration.

Or think of the servant in the parable in Matthew 18. He asked for pity, not forgiveness. But the king—an illustration of the forgiving God—offered him forgiveness, a gift so radical he never really understood it. Clearly he was given forgiveness without repentance. Unfortunately, it was a gift he never opened himself to receive.

Our best example of all is Jesus Himself, who further defined
His new principle of forgiveness when on the cross He said,
"Father, forgive these people [and all who come after them],
because they don't know what they are doing" (Luke 23:34). There
was no repentance by those who crucified Jesus. Yet Jesus asked the
Father to forgive them.

This principle was understood very early in the Church. We
see the same principle at work in Acts 7:60, when Stephen is being
stoned to death because of what his Jewish listeners considered to
be blasphemy. As he is about to die, he shouts, "'Lord, don't
charge them with this sin!' And with that, he died." He fulfills one
condition of Jewish teaching on forgiveness—as the one being
murdered; only he can forgive those sinning against him. But he
also demonstrates that repentance is not a requirement of forgiveness, for those stoning him, including the young man Saul,
who is standing by witnessing what is happening, are certainly
not showing any spirit of repentance. This is part of Jesus' radical
teaching on forgiveness.

Some who contributed to Wiesenthal's book understood the
radical nature of Jesus' teaching on forgiveness but did not agree
with it. They believed that it is a dangerous teaching that eventually makes light of the offense. Martin E. Marty, professor of religious history at the University of Chicago and senior editor of the
Christian Century, wrote,

Is there any kind of situation in which the offense is so gross
and enormous that I should withhold forgiveness in the
face of what appears to be true penitence? My answer would
be that in every circumstance that I can picture, more value
would grow out of forgiveness than out of its withholding.
But I must ask what am I afraid of or concerned about, and
what is it that causes me to hem and hedge, to shuffle and
clear my throat, to be suspicious of that answer?[10]

Marty went on to explain his concern about "cheap grace," wherein one might forgive too easily and let murderers and haters off the hook. He was also concerned that, if forgiveness is freely given, crimes against a people will be taken less seriously.

Prager agreed, saying, "The Christian doctrine of forgiveness has blunted Christian anger at those who oppress them; the notion that one should pray for one's enemies has been taken to mean 'pray for them, do not fight them.'"

In other words, the world cannot survive the easy forgiveness of Christians. But as with cheap grace, cheap forgiveness disappears as a concept when one considers the price Jesus paid for our forgiveness. Genuine unconditional forgiveness flows out of an awareness of the tremendous price that was paid so that we could not only be forgiven but also be forgiving.

So then, why do we want to hold on to the old way of forgiving? Perhaps it is just familiar, or maybe it's because it seems to make better sense—it's more logical to forgive when there's been repentance. However, Jesus calls us to a higher and deeper level of forgiving. We are to forgive even our enemies, simply as an act of obedience, and our ability to forgive in that way flows out of our gratitude for what we have been forgiven.

QUESTIONS TO CONSIDER

1. How would you have responded to the SS man and his request for forgiveness?
2. Why do you think the world cannot understand unconditional forgiveness?
3. What is the hardest thing for you to accept about the idea of being an unconditional forgiver?

CHOOSING TO FORGIVE: FALSE PATHS WE CAN TAKE

The first time I visited Paris, I went to the monument of the deportation of the French who had died in German concentration camps. I was horrified by the inscription over the main door.

"Let us forgive but never let us forget."

All of a sudden I realized that the real virtue came in forgiving precisely while remembering. If I could forget, I would not have to forgive. It would not even be necessary.

VIRGIL ELIZONDO[1]

It's time now to look at how we can actually forgive what seems to be unforgivable. As we do, it's important to remember that our ability to forgive flows out of our awareness of our own forgiveness by God. The more we understand how much we've been forgiven, the more we are able to forgive.

The process always begins in the same place, with the offense that causes us hurt. But where the process goes from there varies, according to the path we follow in handling what has happened. The process of forgiving can even be short-circuited, with the result that we end up in a place of *un*forgiveness—in terms of healing, a dead end. This chapter will examine two common variations of just how this happens.

THE PATH OF DENIAL

The first path available to us is a short one (see figure 1). It begins with the offense, when I experience hurt. When we face a choice about what we are going to do about the offense, we enter into either denial or self-blame.

If we head down the Path of Denial, at this point we will do one of two things. Either e will deny that the hurt occurred at all or we will blame ourselves for what happened. Either one is an absolute—a dichotomy: We do one or the other but not both.

Several years ago I was working with a middle-aged man, whom we'll call Mark. He had come to therapy to work on his marriage but now was trying to come to terms with some very painful experiences he had had with his father. Not only had they occurred during the whole time he was growing up, but they had also continued to the present time. Mark couldn't even be around his father without his father saying or doing something that was extremely hurtful. This seemed to be the older man's normal way of operating, because he did the same thing with each of his kids, as well as with their spouses and even the grandchildren. He was

FIGURE 1

The Path of Denial

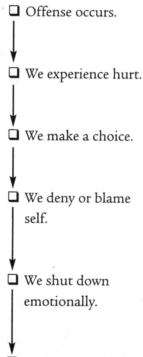

❑ Offense occurs.

❑ We experience hurt.

❑ We make a choice.

❑ We deny or blame self.

❑ We shut down emotionally.

❑ We become depressed.

If we head down the Path of Denial,

at this point we will do one of two things.

Either we will deny that the

hurt occurred at all or we will blame

ourselves for what happened.

clearly, by Mark's own admission, a cruel, mean old man, and had been for as long as Mark could remember.

If we were to chart Mark's process, we could begin with multiple offenses that had occurred over the years. He could easily recall the hurts he had experienced as a result of his father's offenses, and he could recount stories illustrating the hurts he had experienced.

We were just beginning this process when Mark stopped coming to therapy. He reported there had been a family emergency with which he had to deal, and he would call and schedule another appointment as soon as possible.

I didn't hear from him for about two years. Then he called, and we scheduled an appointment. After "catching up" on the family emergency issue, I asked how he had been doing with his father. He told me that about a year earlier his father had died. I expressed my sympathy, and then we talked some about how he had handled his father's death, how it had happened, and how his mother was doing.

Then I got more specific, wanting to know more about the impact of his father's death in light of the painful issues we had been talking about two years earlier. His response shocked me.

"What problems?" he asked me. "My father was a wonderful man. I don't know what you're talking about."

I was taken aback and started to recheck my notes, wondering if I had remembered incorrectly. But, no, there in the notes were some of the things he had said about his father and some of the hurts he had experienced and described to me. He was the same man, but suddenly his father seemed to have become someone else. Nothing I could say, including quoting what he had told me two years earlier, changed his opinion about his father at this time. His father had become a wonderful man who now had never done the things we had talked about earlier. No longer would he tell of the pain he had experienced in his relationship with his dad. He now bypassed that step and moved to denial.

Mark had chosen the Path of Denial. We never did get past that point, and I didn't see Mark after that one session, though I could predict what would happen to him over time—depression and emotional deadness.

Other forms of denial are seen in the attitude, "It's no big deal—no problem at all." We minimize what has happened to us and then dismiss the offense as "no big deal." We may tell ourselves that we understand why the person did what he or she did. We may say we know what that person has gone through in life, so what can you expect from someone like that? Forget about it; it's no problem.

Other times we may dismiss the person as well as the offense. We make light of what was done to us, refusing to acknowledge the pain we have felt, but internally we have cut the offender out of our life. We stop talking to or even about that person. If the offender notices and makes a connection between what we are doing and the offense he or she did, and comes to us to apologize, we are likely to continue to minimize the offense, even with the offender.

Emotional Shutdown

When we choose the Path of Denial, we move to a place of emotional shutdown—the only way, in fact, that we can maintain our denial. We don't want any thing, any feeling, or any person reminding us of what we are denying.

An interesting thing about denial is that its main purpose is to protect us from the truth. I used to think that people in denial were trying to fool me. And they *are* doing that to some degree. However, denial's main purpose is to fool oneself. We choose denial because we cannot face the truth. Perhaps we are protecting the other person to some degree, but we are mostly protecting ourselves from having to deal with the pain of what actually happened.

Depression

Once a person begins to shut down emotionally, he or she must become much more selective about the people he or she hangs around with. This person can't afford to be with people who remind him or her of the past pain or be with people who know too much about those past experiences.

It wasn't too long until Mark left his wife and cut off contact with his children. The next step was to leave the area, find a different wife and start a new life without remembrances of his painful past. That sounds like it might work, but it didn't for Mark. He became depressed, and the new hurt of being cut off from his children served only to remind him of the hurt and pain he had experienced with his father. Hopefully, the pain of his depression and the pain of his isolation from his children will at some point become strong enough that he will choose to face his past and the past he's created, and take the path that leads to forgiveness.

Self-Blame Leads to the Same Result as Denial

Another way someone can head down the Path of Denial is to get caught up in the cycle of self-blame: The entire problem is my fault. I am the reason why you did all those hurtful things to me. I deserved it. What makes this another way to take the Path of Denial is that self-blame itself is a form of denial, since it considers just one absolute: It is *all* my fault. I take it *all* upon myself. I have resolved the problem by taking 100 percent of the blame. There's nothing more to discuss. Case closed. This is nothing more than another way to live in the world of denial.

I spoke with a young woman who had grown up listening to constant criticism from both of her parents. When we started talking about the painful experiences of her childhood, she was quick to say, "But it was my fault. I was bad." Regardless of what we discussed, her response was always the same: "It was my fault." With that kind of attitude, there could be little discussion because the case had already been settled, blame has been assigned, and she had to go on with life as it was.

Those on the Path of Denial who begin with self-blame still end up taking the next step, deadening their emotions. They might say they do feel emotions, but what they actually experience is self-loathing. Because it is such a distortion, it cannot be a true feeling. It is a pseudofeeling that sets a trap. They cannot change because they refuse to change how they view themselves. If they were not completely at fault, then the event at issue would have to be someone else's fault. For some reason, they can't handle that truth. Perhaps they feel some sense of control over the issue by being at fault. If it were someone else's fault, then they wouldn't have any control over the situation. So they shut down their true feelings. And whenever they do that, the end result will always be despair and depression.

THE PATH OF BITTERNESS

The Path of Bitterness (see figure 2) begins just like the Path of Denial. There is an offense that results in hurt. We tell and retell the story; then we make a choice. People tend to choose the Path of Bitterness when they get caught up with wanting to understand the reasons for the offense. They think, if only they could understand *why* the other person did what he or she did, they could get over it and let it go.

Accused or Excused

In their search for understanding, those who choose this path often vacillate between *accusing* the other for the wrong he or she

FIGURE 2
The Path of Bitterness

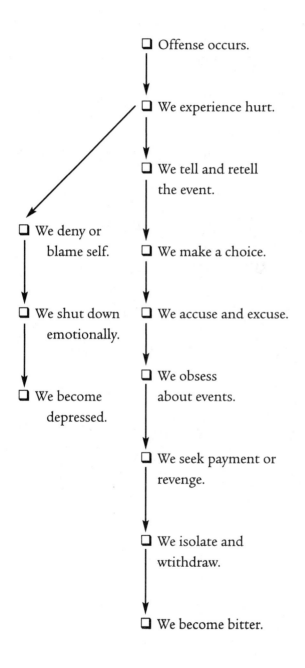

❑ Offense occurs.

❑ We experience hurt.

❑ We tell and retell
the event.

❑ We deny or
blame self.

❑ We make a choice.

❑ We shut down
emotionally.

❑ We accuse and excuse.

❑ We become
depressed.

❑ We obsess
about events.

❑ We seek payment or
revenge.

❑ We isolate and
wtithdraw.

❑ We become bitter.

People tend to choose the Path of Bitterness when they get caught up with wanting to understand the reasons for the offense. They think, if only they could understand why the other person did what he or she did, they could get over it and let it go.

has done and trying to *excuse* that person for the wrong. There must be a reason, they tell themselves, and so they search for new information that would supposedly help resolve the issue. Although they may get new information that seems to clearly prove the other person guilty of the offense, there is still enough doubt to lead to a continued search. More information comes, and it seems to partially excuse the other person, but the pain remains. Back and forth they go between excusing and accusing in a self-perpetuating cycle.

Obsessed with the Event

Eventually the need to understand will lead to an obsession with the hurtful event. Sharon is an example of what can happen when one is driven by the need to understand something that really can never be fully understood. She and her husband Jack came to counseling about two years after Sharon discovered that he was having an affair. When Sharon confronted Jack, he immediately confessed and broke off the other relationship completely. It was almost as though he had been relieved to have been "found out."

As is often the case, Jack was so full of guilt that he answered every one of Sharon's questions, giving her far more details than she needed to know. The more she knew, the more she needed to deal with in her memory, but that didn't stop her. She wanted to know *why* Jack had done such a hurtful thing, and Jack never had a very satisfying answer for her.

Since Jack couldn't come up with good enough reasons why he'd had the affair, Sharon had lunch with the other woman. She had a list of questions and again got far more information than she could possibly process without a tremendous amount of additional hurt. Eventually she had lunch with the other woman again and asked some new questions. Again, the woman's responses never even came close to answering the "why" Sharon was desperately seeking. When Jack would try to get her to let go of the matter, she would think he was simply trying to excuse his own behavior. Eventually Jack learned simply to keep quiet.

Sharon finally decided she and Jack needed to come to marriage counseling. She hoped the marriage counselor would be able to help her understand why Jack had done such a terrible thing. At first I tried to answer Sharon's questions, but nothing I said really satisfied her. Finally I told her she was on an impossible search. There can never be a satisfactory answer as to why a spouse cheats on his or her marriage. Even so, I was beginning to feel sorry for Jack. For almost four years he had paid a tremendous price for his foolish and stupid behavior. But Sharon was stuck on a path that led to nowhere but more pain.

The Issue of Shame

Sharon's behavior could be interpreted as a way to get even with Jack, but I don't believe that was her motivation. What would have motivated her for more than four years to keep searching, to keep the spotlight on Jack? Sharon may have been motivated by the shame she had experienced as a result of Jack's affair. As irrational as it may seem, the betrayed partner often struggles with self-blame. There's often a total confusion of responsibility for what has taken place. The one betrayed believes that he or she has somehow failed as a spouse, causing his or her partner to turn to someone else.

As long as Sharon searched for the answer in Jack, she didn't have to acknowledge her haunting feelings about herself. She didn't have to face questions like, "How have I failed so badly as a wife that my husband had to look elsewhere for satisfaction?" or "Why wasn't I good enough to keep him home?" These shameful thoughts could be kept away from her awareness if she continued to focus solely on understanding why Jack had messed up so badly.

Though sometimes an obsession with understanding the event serves more than one purpose, until Sharon became willing to look at these shame issues, she would become increasingly entrenched on the path that just leads to bitterness.

Eventually the feelings of shame grow stronger, and require more effort on our part to keep them comfortably away. This means the search for reasons can too easily escalate into seeking revenge.

Seeking Payment/Revenge

An obsession with the painful event can lead eventually to a demand for payment of the debt owed.

Recently I spoke with a couple that seemed to have entered counseling because of an affair the wife had had two years earlier. It took some time to learn about the rest of the story. We had been making good progress when suddenly something triggered the wife's anger toward her husband because of an affair he'd had 10 years earlier. He then got angry with her for "bringing that up again," and soon they were both out of control.

Once we had calmed everything down, I realized we were dealing with two affairs rather than one. Whenever we seemed to be making progress, one of them would explode about what the other had done and they were back to a heated discussion about who had hurt whom the worst.

This couple had taken the Path of Denial regarding the husband's affair 10 years earlier, but deeply buried hurts and resentments easily flooded to the surface whenever the couple tried to deal with the wife's more recent affair. They claimed they wanted to forgive one other, but each time they came close to beginning the process of forgiveness, one or the other would dig in his or her heels, caught up in seeking payment for past hurts and refusing to cancel any debts from the other person's past.

Isolation/Withdrawal

Eventually this couple separated and withdrew, not only from each other, but from their circle of friends as well. They were embarrassed that a process at which they had started out doing so well had failed so miserably.

But there is also something about choosing the Path of Bitterness that leads to isolation and aloneness. When we become obsessed with a hurtful event in our lives and we cannot or will not let it heal, we push other people away from us. We become so absorbed in our own process that we no longer seem to care about what is going on in someone else's life. We become self-centered—or "hurtful-event-centered." Either way leaves no room for anyone else in our lives, and by the time we realize what has happened, we may be too angry and too hurt even to care.

The Place of Bitterness

There's only one place to go at this point, and that's to the place of bitterness. Why would anyone want to go there? Actually, it's all too easy to do. The feelings of bitterness can so easily be justified.

If Sharon realizes at some point that she has wasted all these years in a fruitless search, she could easily say, "Well, I have a right to be bitter. He violated our marriage, and everything I did was an attempt to right that wrong. It didn't work. I guess all men are the same. They're all worthless and not to be trusted! Who wouldn't be bitter over that?" She might feel justified in her feelings, but the truth is, she will have become a slave to the past if that happens. She will be in bondage to the hurtful event, and her life will have become so much less than what God meant it to be. She will never know what she could have experienced if she had chosen to work on through to forgiveness.

Moreover, the Bible reminds us that the place of bitterness affects the others in our lives as well. Hebrews 12:15 says that wherever bitterness "springs up, many are corrupted by its poison." Jack probably lives in the place of bitterness now—along with his children and some friends.

However, we don't have to take either of these paths. There is a third option. We can take the Path of Forgiveness, which we will be exploring in the next chapter.

QUESTIONS TO CONSIDER

1. What events have you denied as being hurtful in your life?

2. Are you caught in a pattern of self-blame, or self-loathing?

3. Is there someone whom you need to forgive, but instead, you are trying to understand why that person did what he or she did?

4. Do you feel bitter toward someone? If so, keep that person in mind as you read the next chapter.

CHAPTER SIX

THE PATH OF
FORGIVENESS

A person will find it cheaper to pardon than to resent.
Forgiveness saves the expense of anger, the cost
of hatred, the waste of spirit.

HANNAH MORE

Fortunately we have a third choice, the Path of Forgiveness (see figure 3). The good news is that there is nothing that occurs in our lives that is too big for us to take this path. Sometimes our pain is so intense that it seems like forgiveness is impossible, but with time, patience and hard work, we can walk down the Path of Forgiveness. The intense journey may seem too long, and the pain more than we can bear, but everything in our past can and must be dealt with through forgiveness.

Once again, this path begins at the same starting point as the other paths. We are the victim of a hurtful offense and experience deep hurt and pain. We tell and retell the story of what happened, but when we come to the point of decision, we move down a different path, one that leads to our being able to forgive even the unforgivable.

PLACE BLAME APPROPRIATELY

Our choice of path is determined by our placement of blame.

As we saw in the last chapter, the Path of Denial begins with either my blaming no one and denying the hurt or with blaming myself. The Path of Bitterness begins with movement back and forth between blaming the other person and trying to find an excusable reason for the behavior. Either of these choices results in short-circuiting our healing process.

You may be surprised to know that the Path of Forgiveness also begins with blaming. However, we now seek an appropriate way to place blame. One could say that we seek to place blame in a very responsible way. At first it may not feel much different from the first stepping-stone on the other pathways. We may begin with denial, self-blame, accusing or excusing behaviors, but our desire is to act responsibly in the placing of blame. This is where it can be very helpful to have the assistance of someone whom we can trust, who will not make matters worse and who

FIGURE 3
The Path of Forgiveness

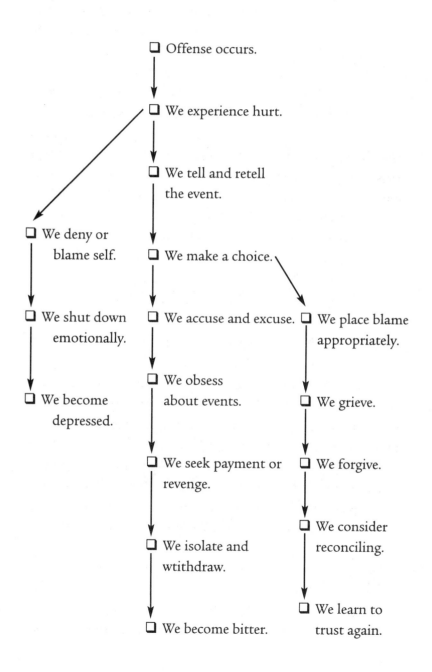

❑ Offense occurs.

❑ We experience hurt.

❑ We tell and retell
the event.

❑ We deny or
blame self.

❑ We make a choice.

❑ We shut down
emotionally.

❑ We accuse and excuse.

❑ We place blame
appropriately.

❑ We become
depressed.

❑ We obsess
about events.

❑ We grieve.

❑ We seek payment or
revenge.

❑ We forgive.

❑ We isolate and
wtithdraw.

❑ We consider
reconciling.

❑ We become bitter.

❑ We learn to
trust again.

will not allow us to get caught up in a mere blame game.

Sometimes fixing the blame seems very clear. For some of the people whose stories we read in the first chapter, the placing of blame was confirmed by a court decision. But at other times, it is not so easy.

How, for instance, does one fix blame when there's been an extramarital affair? Some say it is always the fault of both spouses, and in some ways, that may be true. It usually takes both people to set the stage for an affair. However, it only takes one person to act on it and actually have the affair. Only one person has crossed the line, and blame needs to be fixed on that person for crossing the line.

What about hurts we experience as children at the hands of our parents or other important adults? Blame clearly belongs to the adult. There can be an added wrinkle, of course. As I was working through my own issues about my father, my only hesitation in blaming him was the fact that he was dead. I had no problem with the idea that he was responsible, however. He was the adult and I was the child.

Not everyone finds this concept that simple, though. Many people I talk with have a tough time blaming their parents. They are convinced they were bad as children and deserved the abuse they suffered.

A child is never responsible for being abused for the simple fact that he or she is the child. That's a safe, sure and predictable principle you can follow. That same principle applies to hurts perpetrated by older siblings. The smaller, less powerful person cannot be to blame for the behavior of the bigger, more powerful person.

One young woman had been repeatedly molested by her older brother when she was between the ages of five and seven, until the parents finally caught him. In her mind, it had been her fault. When pressed to explain how something like that could have been her fault, she said, "I danced provocatively in front of him when I was five." Over the years she had developed this irrational but powerful belief that supported placing the blame on herself. When I rather forcefully reminded her that a five-year-old doesn't even know the meaning of the word "provocative," she finally began to see where the blame belonged—on her older brother. The process of true forgiveness always includes our placing appropriate blame where it belongs, as well as placing blame on ourselves when it is appropriate.

GRIEVE

An essential step in the forgiveness process is that we grieve what has been lost. With every serious offense that occurs in our life, something is lost. When I dealt with my father issues, I needed to grieve for the things my father was that he shouldn't have been in my life, and for what he never was that he should have been. Twenty years after my father's death, I was finally able to grieve.

Irene, whose situation we discussed in the first chapter, had to grieve for two lives that were never realized, and Judy grieved for a marriage that would never be quite the same, even after she and her husband experienced healing together. Nelson Mandela grieved the loss of 27 years of freedom. Corrie ten Boom grieved for the years she lost while in the concentration camps. Mark needed to be able to grieve for the kind of father he so desperately wanted and needed but couldn't or wouldn't have.

Every painful offense involves a loss of some kind that can only be processed through grief. What does it mean to grieve? A simple way to understand grief in the forgiveness process is to describe it by its stages. It begins with denial and ends with acceptance. These two stages of grief are like bookends that hold the process together.

Between the bookends, the beginning and end of grief, we (1) are angry and protest the wrong, and (2) experience sadness and resignation over what was lost. We don't do these two things in any definite or predictable order—first one and then the other and that's it. In fact, we typically bounce back and forth between anger and sadness, but both must be experienced for us to grieve successfully.

At the time of my father's death, I did not grieve. I didn't feel angry, and I couldn't feel sad. I tried at times, but I wasn't able to grieve. At the funeral home, I had moments when I cried slightly, but it was more an attempt to meet social expectations than an authentic expression of grief. In the 20 years that followed, I didn't grieve his death. I didn't grieve over his life, either. I had taken the Path of Denial. When I finally was able to begin to grieve the loss of my father, it started with my getting in touch with my anger. I didn't experience the sadness of that loss until I was near the end of the process, but my sadness was necessary as well.

Irene could only get angry with herself. But that kind of anger wasn't part of the grieving process. It was taking her on the Path of Denial. Whenever Irene talked about her abortions, she experienced sadness for a short time, but then she used self-blame and self-loathing to shut herself down. Since she could only experience briefly that one facet of grieving, she wasn't able to complete the process and remained stuck with her sadness.

Judy's experience was different from Irene's. At first Judy was so overwhelmed by her anger at her husband that her feelings of sadness were few and fleeting. But she couldn't stay in the place of anger, and soon she was overwhelmed by sadness. Since she had access to both anger and sadness, she moved forward in the process of actually forgiving her husband.

TYPES OF ANGER

Anger may well be the most misunderstood emotion. For all the trouble anger can cause, you'd think we'd work harder to understand it, but we don't.

Our understanding of anger is complicated by how we define it. Our childhood experiences of anger in our own families color how we understand it later in life. Those who grew up in a family with a tyrannical parent usually equate all forms of anger with rage. Often these individuals follow their parent's pattern, believing that rage is just a normal part of life. On the other hand, some may struggle with or try to avoid any angry feelings at all, for fear of becoming a tyrant like their parent, or simply from a general fear of anger.

Others may have had the opposite experience. Their parents never raised their voices, but now ordinary impatience is labeled as anger. These individuals are extremely sensitive to anything that even smells like anger, both in themselves and in others. The slightest raising of the voice can set off fear of being out of control.

Anger is a primary emotion that can include everything from cold silence to mild impatience to an out-of-control rage. Whatever word you use to describe that range of emotion is what we mean here when we use the word "anger."

An interesting phenomenon about anger is that, when we experience this emotion, either in healthy ways or unhealthy ways, we often feel stronger. One of the roles of healthy anger is to protect us in certain situations. It can help stop a process in which someone has previously victimized us. Anger protests, "You cannot continue to do this to me!" The absence of anger when we are the victims of someone else's behavior leaves us feeling weak, exposed and helpless.

Not all anger is productive, however. Expressions of our anger can be harmful to us and to others. The apostle Paul warned us to be careful about our anger. He said, "And 'don't sin by letting anger gain control over you.' Don't let the sun go down while you are still angry, for anger gives a mighty foothold

An interesting phenomenon about anger is that, when we experience this emotion, either in healthy ways or unhealthy ways, we often feel stronger.

to the Devil" (Eph. 4:26). Obviously, Paul believed there is a way to be angry that leads to sin and a way to be angry that doesn't. There is an anger that is only concerned with our self-absorbed, self-centered issues and really doesn't care about the other person. There is also self-directed anger, which is anger directed at oneself and is an expression of our not caring anything about ourselves. Healthy anger involves a concern with justice, with protecting both you and me, and is disciplined in its actions.

Becoming angry too quickly can be counterproductive in the forgiveness process. Solomon warned, "Those who are short-tempered do foolish things. . . . Those who control their anger have great understanding; those with a hasty temper will make mistakes" (Prov. 14:17,29). In Proverbs 19:11 he added, "People with good sense restrain their anger." James likewise said, "My dear brothers and sisters, be quick to listen, slow to speak, and slow to get angry. Your anger can never make things right in God's sight" (Jas. 1:19-20).

Being disciplined in our anger and cautious in its expression does not mean that we deny our anger, however. Healthy anger is essential to the forgiveness process. In fact, if we try to forgive without experiencing anger, we are not really forgiving; we are merely trying to *excuse* the behavior.

When someone has hurt us, there is usually nothing to be gained by getting angry directly with the other person, especially if the hurt took place a long time ago. In my situation, confronting my father wasn't an option, so I was free to be angry and had no thought of confronting my father. Even if he had been alive, however, there would have been nothing gained for me by expressing my anger with him in a face-to-face meeting, or even indirectly in a letter. The purpose of my anger was to grieve, not to confront. In fact, confrontation should come only after we have finished the process of actually forgiving the other person.

It's important to remember that the forgiving process we are describing is something a person does internally, without the other person's involvement. In fact, it may even be helpful to limit any contact we have with the person that we are seeking to forgive.

Someone once asked me, "What if I am trying to forgive this person in my life, but he [or she] keeps doing the same thing to me? How am I supposed to forgive in that situation?" In a situation like that we must first do what we can to stop the hurtful behavior, perhaps by limiting any contact with the other person until we have become strong enough to protect ourselves. Then we can work on forgiveness.

SADNESS

The other facet of grieving is the experience of sadness. Our heart may have been broken by our loss and tears become our constant companion. But sadness is more than just tears. Other things are going on inside us as well.

During the angry facet of grief, we are focused on the other person and how they hurt us. During the sadness facet, we become more focused on ourselves. We go through a period of self-evaluation, considering what has been lost to us. What is it that we will never experience again? What has been taken away that we can never regain? What has been our part in the process?

We experience a growing sense of resignation as we journey into the depths of our sadness. There is something healing in our tears. Sometimes we get a sense of the experience from the perspective of the other person. We put ourselves in his or her shoes, and in doing so, we realize that we are both sinners who have been forgiven by a gracious God and that they have also lost something through this event.

As stated earlier, men seem to have great difficulty with the sadness aspect of grief. Not only is it hard for men to cry but we also seem to avoid the self-evaluation that typically goes along with the experience of sadness. This is a time of reflection, not a time of action. Men typically feel an urgent need to take action to solve the problem, but we need to resist this urge and learn to sit with our sadness. King Solomon reminded us that "There is a time for everything. . . . A time to cry and a time to laugh. A time to grieve and a time to dance" (Ecc. 3:1,4). Men need to take the time to cry and grieve.

As we journey down the Path of Forgiveness, we need to remember that reaching the place of forgiving requires that we experience both the anger and the sadness. Once we have spent time in both, we are free to move on to the next step on the path, which is where we take action and actually forgive the one who hurt us so deeply.

FORGIVE

We will typically bounce back and forth between anger and sadness during our grieving, and we may do this until we are almost worn out by the process. That's why it is usually important to have someone we trust walking with us on the Path of Forgiveness. We need someone to say to us, "It's time. You've grieved enough. You need to forgive." When we get to that point, we move from what has been a process to making the actual decision to finally and completely forgive.

People sometimes argue about whether forgiveness is a process or a decision. When we are dealing with things that feel unforgivable, it is definitely both—a process that takes time and a decision at a particular point in time. In fact, it is two decisions, the first being to actually take the Path of Forgiveness.

Up to the point of making that second decision, to forgive, we have been on a journey. For some minor offenses, the process may take only a moment before we make the decision to forgive.

But when we are dealing with issues that seem unforgivable, the process may take several years before we are able to come to the decisive point of actually forgiving.

A friend of mine is on the staff at the Cleveland Rescue Mission. Peter Bliss has developed a program that he calls a "Debt Canceling Forum." After doing several of these, he called me one day to ask permission to use material from my earlier book on forgiveness, titled *Forgiving our Parents, Forgiving Ourselves.* I was honored that he had found the material helpful and asked him to tell me about his work. We talked a while, and then I asked when the next forum was scheduled. It was on a weekend I would be in Cleveland, and we made arrangements so I could attend.

At the mission, Peter works with men who have become tired of a lifestyle of alcoholism, of living on the streets, or of repeated prison sentences. They go through a yearlong program to get on stable ground and be prepared to become productive citizens. The Debt Canceling Forum is optional, but most of the men choose to participate each time it is offered. On the particular Saturday when I was present, some of the women from the women's program were also in attendance.

Peter spent the first morning laying a foundation for understanding forgiveness. He equated the debts in our lives with our unmet needs and talked about what we typically do with these needs. Peter showed these people how their addictions, their anger toward themselves, and their judgmental attitudes resulted from their not properly taking care of their unmet needs. Then he talked about breaking through their own denial and actually forgiving those who had not met their needs, their parents in particular.

The myths of forgiveness were discussed, and questions were answered. Men who had already taken the forum helped answer the questions of the newcomers. And they knew the answers.

Finally, at the end of the morning, Peter challenged everyone there to write a letter of unconditional forgiveness for one or both parents, and to return Sunday morning prepared to read the letter to an empty chair (or chairs) in front of the group. During the break, I spoke with another member of the mission staff and asked her why she was there. She told me about a man named Louis, who prior to the last Debt Canceling Forum had been a cause for concern among the staff. He had been in the program for about six weeks but didn't seem to be making any connections with anyone else. He was quiet and withdrawn, even from the staff. She said he was that way when she had left on Friday, but when she came in on Monday morning, Louis was a totally different person. He was smiling and talking to others in the program. He was so animated that she went up to him and asked, "What happened to you?"

"Oh, I went to 'debt canceling' this past weekend," he answered.

She knew that Peter had done this weekend program several times, but she had no idea what went on. All Louis could say to her was "I forgave my parents—it was incredible!" So this woman had to come and see for herself what went on.

During the Sunday morning session, which I wasn't able to attend, each of the men and women got up in front of the group, read his or her letter of unconditional forgiveness, and then walked over to a silver urn and burned the letter. It was a ritual that firmly implanted in their experience the reality of their act of forgiving.

I asked Peter later why these men and women didn't need to take the time to grieve over what they were forgiving. His answer was that most of their lives they had been acting out their grief. They had certainly expressed their anger, and for many of them it had led to prison. And when you've hit bottom, you have plenty of time to experience the sadness of your place in life. "No," he said, "they have already done the grief work. What they needed to do at this time was the act of forgiving."

Since that conversation with Peter, I have had the privilege of teaching on forgiveness in several Youth With A Mission (YWAM) schools. During the first four days of the week we look at all aspects of forgiveness, and on Thursday, each of the class members is asked to write a letter to the person they need to forgive. They often write angry letters at first, and I encourage them to do so. Then they are to write out a one-paragraph summary of the hurt they have experienced, followed by this statement: "Because through Jesus' death on the cross I have been forgiven, I am now unconditionally forgiving you for what you have done."

On Friday morning the students come together, bringing their letters. We usually have a big cooking pot and a book of matches ready. Each student begins by setting up the appropriate number of chairs. Then, standing in front of the group, he or she reads the paragraph and the words of forgiveness to the empty chairs. Following that, the student moves to the cooking pot and burns the letter, much as churches have burned mortgages that are paid in full. It's one thing to talk about the process of forgiveness and quite another to actually take the step and publicly offer unconditional forgiveness to the one who has hurt you. That's the decisive aspect of forgiving.

I remember one young man from another culture who forgave his father. His father had been physically abusive to him all through the years he had been living at home. That morning the young man read what he had written in his native language, which only a few of the students understood. He wept, sometimes uncontrollably, as he first read his letter and then offered his father unconditional forgiveness for what had been done to him over the years. A year later, I saw this young man at another school. He was a different person. God had used his act of forgiveness to free him from the bondage of his hurtful past, enabling him to become the man God intended him to be. He was another Louis.

When we do such a decisive act of forgiveness, it is helpful to have a ritual that we can look back to as a marker. When the Israelites came into the Promised Land, God told them to build markers to commemorate the great things God was going to do in the land through them. The burning of the letter becomes a marker. It's a stone in the ground that we can point to and say, "I have forgiven that awful hurt!"

How long should we wait before we forgive? That's hard to say because it depends a lot on the depth of our hurt. But the act of forgiveness always comes before we think we are fully ready. That's why it helps to have a trusted friend who can wisely say, "It's time to forgive." Part of us may protest and say that we need more time to grieve. In fact, the act of forgiving seems to come just before we feel we are ready, but when we look back, we realize we were ready.

One additional and very important point must be noted. Once I have forgiven someone of the offense, I have given up the right ever to use that offense against him or her in any way. Not only have I given up my right to get even, or to demand payment, but also I have given up my right to "hold it over them." Forgiveness means the offense is gone. I may remember the offense, but I will "remember it *against them* no more!" Even if at some later time that person hurts me again, the present offense is a dead issue! I have given up the right to use it against them, *ever!*

CONSIDER RECONCILIATION

As both Christians and members of a family, we live in community. We don't live in isolation. Even though forgiveness is something we do on our own, we can hope for reconciliation.

However, when dealing with what seem like unforgivable situations, we need to be very careful in considering reconciliation.

When we truly forgive, the other person doesn't owe us anything anymore; we have canceled the debt. I don't think we can ever approach the other person without *any* expectations, but after forgiving, our expectations are low. Since the other person owes us nothing, that's what we can expect—nothing. If something good does happen, it is like a gift. If nothing good happens, we are not too disappointed, since our expectations are minimal.

As we noted earlier, genuine reconciliation can only take place when both the offender and the offended have entered into a forgiveness process. If only the offended, the one hurt, is in that process, there can be no reconciliation.

If we desire reconciliation and decide we want to begin what must be a bilateral process, we must test for the possibility. We may do this by observing the other person carefully, much like Joseph did when his brothers came to him for food. We may also reach out cautiously by beginning a dialogue that is loosely related to the issue but not directly connected to it. If we find that the other person has been struggling with what he or she did, and is experiencing godly sorrow over the hurt he or she caused, we can move forward and work through the healing and reconciling.

But reconciliation is always an *option*, not a requirement. We are not required as an act of obedience to reconcile. We are required as an act of obedience to forgive.

LEARN TO TRUST AGAIN

Most seemingly unforgivable events take place in a relationship with someone we are close to and care about. Prior to the hurtful event, we trusted that person. But trust is something that can be destroyed in a moment, in a singular act, and one of the losses we experience is our trust in that person.

Judy had trusted her husband for years, but the revelation of his infidelity instantly destroyed her trust for him. Can she ever trust him again? Yes, but it will be a long, slow process that will require a very open, repentant attitude on the part of her husband.

It takes the willingness of the offending party to rebuild trust. The genuineness of the godly sorrow on the part of the offender will create an openness that says, "I know you don't trust me anymore. I want you to learn to trust me again, and I will do *whatever* you need me to do to help you learn to trust me. And I am willing to do this for as long as you need me to." Without that kind of open attitude, trust becomes impossible to rebuild. One person alone (and especially not the one who was offended) cannot rebuild trust in a broken relationship. It takes the willingness of both parties, but especially that of the offending party, to rebuild trust.

The journey along the Path of Forgiveness isn't easy. In many ways it will feel like an uphill climb. It goes against the grain in so many ways. How much easier it is simply to say, "Let them pay. They did the wrong!" When we take the Path of Forgiveness, however, we repudiate revenge and let go of our desire to get even. Forgiveness requires that we accept the undeserved. Even though it isn't fair, that's what Jesus expects us to do.

Near the end of the movie *The Prince of Tides*, the main character, Tom Wingo, is sitting in the bleachers of the high school stadium and reflecting back on all the chaos we have just watched, the chaotic dysfunction of the family he grew up in and the chaos in his own family. I found his words to himself exciting because they were profoundly biblical: "I've learned that there is nothing that happens in family that is beyond forgiveness." They were in great contrast to what we had just watched because it had been so "sinful."

The same line appeared in Pat Conroy's book, to which the movie was faithful. But Conroy could have had Tom Wingo go further by saying, "There is nothing in life that is beyond forgiveness." Then he would have captured even better what Jesus expects of each of us.

Forgiveness is a way of life that Jesus calls us to live. Paul summed up what Jesus wants of us when he wrote, "Get rid of all bitterness, rage, anger, harsh words, and slander, as well as all types of malicious behavior. Instead, be kind to each other, tenderhearted, forgiving one another as God through Christ has forgiven you" (Eph. 4:31-32).

QUESTIONS TO CONSIDER

1. What are some of the reasons that you have resisted the Path of Forgiveness in the past?
2. In your experience, what has been the hardest part of grieving?
3. Make a list of some of the people you have forgiven over the years. Who was the hardest one to forgive? Why?

CHAPTER SEVEN

FORGIVING OURSELVES

*Forgiveness is never complete until, first, we have
experienced the forgiveness of God, second, we can forgive others who
have wronged us, and third, we are able to forgive ourselves.*

CHARLES STANLEY

Iremember when my book *Forgiving Our Parents, Forgiving Ourselves* was first published. Several of my colleagues wanted to get into a theological discussion with me over what they believed was an absurdity, forgiving myself. We had several animated discussions, with neither party giving any ground to the other. Inwardly, I recognized their point. Only God can truly forgive us for the wrongs we have done. I wasn't concerned with the theological issue of our forgiving ourselves, however; I was thinking about a man we'll call Ray.

Ray had been a mean, crotchety husband for years. His wife had finally grown tired of his behavior and left him. During the first several years afterward they worked out a friendship and Ray mellowed. But there was no way his wife was going to trust that he had truly changed and move back in with him.

I listened as he described his behavior. I could see that he had been mean and would have been extremely hard to live with. Then he spoke of forgiveness.

"I've asked my wife at least 100 times to forgive me," he said.

"Has she forgiven you?"

"She says she has, but she still doesn't trust me to be different."

"What else have you done?" I asked him.

"I've begged God to forgive me and to truly change me."

"Has He?" I responded.

"Well," he said hesitantly. "I think in my head that He has, but down in the depths of me I don't think so." Then he quickly added, "I know He's promised to forgive everything we've ever done, so yes, He's supposed to have forgiven me. I guess the real problem is that *I* can't forgive me."

I don't know how many people have said that to me throughout my years as a counselor. Intellectually they have the facts down correctly. They can quote 1 John 1:9 as quickly as I can: "But if we confess our sins to him, he is faithful and just to forgive us and to cleanse us from every wrong." All the same, they get hung up on the issue of forgiving themselves.

Eventually I developed a standard response, meant only to make them think. It usually works. I say something to this effect: "I find it interesting that you have higher standards for forgiveness than God does. He can forgive you, but you can't forgive you. How is that possible?"

Anyone who has sinned boldly, or is highly sensitive to sin in his or her life, will struggle with forgiving himself or herself. It is not pride, nor is it a weakness, that we accept God's forgiveness *and* hold on to an attitude of unforgiveness toward ourselves. It is a sensitive spirit that holds us back.

JUDAS AND PETER

To understand the process of forgiving ourselves, let's look at the example of two of Jesus' disciples—both of whom betrayed their Lord. Judas, we know as the ultimate betrayer. For 30 pieces of silver, he turned Jesus over to those who wanted Him dead. There are some who think Judas did this with the intention of "helping" Jesus set up an earthly kingdom. When that effort failed, Judas gave in to his shame and feelings of guilt. Whether true or not, in bitterness Judas returned the money and then went out and hanged himself. He didn't think forgiveness was possible.

In contrast, consider the disciple Peter. He had told Jesus that he was ready to go to prison with Him, even to die for Him. Jesus predicted, however, that Peter would betray Him three times before the very next morning. And just as Peter denied even knowing Jesus for the third time, "the rooster crowed. At that moment the Lord turned and looked at Peter. Then Peter remembered that the Lord had said, 'Before the rooster crows tomorrow morning, you will deny me three times.' And Peter left the courtyard, crying bitterly" (Luke 22:60-62).

For several days Peter was left with the pain of his failure and sinfulness. For him to become the great apostle, Peter had to learn to forgive himself, and Jesus helped him in that process. Instead of isolating himself, as Judas did, Peter made certain he was with the other disciples. He was back at work fishing with six of the other disciples (see John 21:1-17). So the first principle we see in Peter's life about forgiving ourselves is this: *Don't isolate—place yourself in the presence of those who love you.* This is what Peter did and what Judas failed to do.

It's easy to imagine how uncomfortable Peter was when he saw Jesus. He didn't expect to meet up with the Savior, but then Jesus had sought them out. He probably ate his breakfast in silence, sitting near the outer edge of the group. He wanted to be there, but a part of him wanted to hide, to isolate himself, just as Judas had. But his being there with the other disciples gave Jesus the opportunity to help Peter forgive himself.

Notice what Jesus does with Peter after they finish breakfast. He approaches Peter and asks him the same question three times— "Peter, do you love Me?" Much has been made about how Jesus asks him three times to offset the three times Peter denied Jesus. And much has been made about the Greek words used by both Peter and Jesus for "love." But I think the principle we want to consider here is that Jesus' questions of Peter forced him to look, not at his guilt and shame over his denial of Jesus, but to look within himself at the great love he had for Jesus, and the great love he felt from Jesus, in spite of his sin. The second principle in forgiving ourselves we find in this passage is this: *You need to put yourself in a place where you are loved and where you can experience being loved.*

But there is more. Each time Peter responded to Jesus' question, Jesus gave him a vision of his future. Peter's shame and guilt is going to be overcome—he is going to experience forgiving himself—by getting back into a place of experiencing love and by looking forward to the future with a confidence that comes from Jesus' commissioning him to a great future. "Feed my sheep," Peter is told. "Don't sit there in your guilt and shame—I have something important for you to do," is what Jesus could have been saying to him. So the third principle we can get from this passage is this: *Do something! Get busy doing something meaningful— something God wants you to do.* Peter does just that—he becomes the one who preaches in Acts 2—the Day of Pentecost. He is the one who opens the gospel to the Gentiles through his interaction with Cornelius in Acts 10. He contributes two books to the canon of the New Testament. He sums up what he learned when he writes, "Now you can have sincere love for each other as brothers and sisters because you were cleansed from your sins when you accepted the truth of the Good News. So see to it that you really do love each other intensely with all your hearts" (1 Pet. 1:22). Peter became the man Jesus knew he could be, and his facing his failure and forgiving himself was an essential part of that process.

PAUL AND STEPHEN

Look also at the experience of the apostle Paul. Prior to his conversion to the Christian faith, Paul had been the great enemy of the Early Church, and of Jesus. He was feared by the early Christians, and rightfully so, for he had the power of life and death over them. Many were put to death because of Paul's instruction. And we have the vivid description of Stephen being stoned to death as the early Paul, then known as Saul, stood by and watched. He "was one of the official witnesses at the killing of Stephen" (Acts 8:1). Paul had much to forgive himself for in his preconversion behavior!

In truth, Paul would have been less than human if, during those silent years after his conversion, he had not struggled with the issue of how to forgive himself for the horrible things he had done against Christ and the church. Perhaps his incredible writings about God's forgiveness came from that struggle. He takes what Jesus taught and puts it into the context of our everyday lives. For example, he urges us to "Get rid of all bitterness, rage, anger, harsh words, and slander, as well as all types of malicious behavior. Instead, be kind to each other, tenderhearted, forgiving one another, just as God through Christ has forgiven you" (Eph. 4:31-32). He doesn't speak directly to the issue of forgiving ourselves, but He understood the power of forgiveness! He could only do that if he had forgiven himself for his past.

PERFORMANCE-BASED LIVING

The main reason so many of us struggle with forgiving ourselves is probably that we believe we need to *earn* forgiveness. While God may freely forgive, we are not as generous. We think we have to earn our forgiveness somehow—we need to be extra good to make up for the horrible thing we did. Peter would have had to earn forgiveness for his betrayal of Jesus, and if he performed well enough over a long enough period of time, he would be able to forgive himself.

As you read the preceding paragraph, it is easy to see how foolish such an idea can be. That is, we can see its foolishness when applied to someone else. However, it still seems to make sense when we think about ourselves. It's all too easy to disappoint ourselves and get caught up in the self-recrimination list in our own minds. At such times we tend to ignore the fact that God doesn't do this when we disappoint Him.

FOCUSING ON OUR BEING FORGIVEN

One thing we struggle with when we need to forgive ourselves is making the distinction between *being* forgiven and *feeling* forgiven. We can know *intellectually* that we have been forgiven, but what we have done is so wrong that, in our minds, we need to earn the right to feel forgiven. How different that is from the good news of Jesus Christ. We cannot earn forgiveness. It is an act of grace—a gift from God. What we need to do at that time is focus in on the reality of the forgiveness we have received from God. We need to focus our thoughts on anything and everything that reinforces the reality of God's grace and forgiveness in our lives.

How can we get to the place where we *feel* forgiven when we have done something terribly wrong in our lives? We focus on the reality of God's forgiveness of us. We meditate on passages of Scripture like the following psalm.

> Praise the Lord, I tell myself; with my whole heart, I will praise his holy name. Praise the Lord, I tell myself, and never forget the good things he does for me. He forgives all my sins and heals all my diseases. He ransoms me from death and surrounds me with love and tender mercies (Ps. 103:1-4).

Or we focus on a passage such as Romans 8, where we begin with the reality that there is nothing in all of life that can condemn us when we are in Christ. And then that great chapter ends with the incredible truth from Paul:

> And I am convinced that nothing can ever separate us from his love. Death can't, and life can't. The angels can't, and the demons can't. Our fears for today, our worries about tomorrow, and even the powers of hell can't keep God's love away. Whether we are high above the sky or in the deepest ocean, nothing in all creation will ever be able to separate us from the love of God that is revealed in Christ Jesus our Lord (Rom. 8:38-39).

How can we get to the place

where we feel forgiven when we

have done something terribly

wrong in our lives?

At the same time, we focus our minds through worship and song on the unfailing love of God for us. I remember a time when I had acted very foolishly, hurting my family and myself. In my own pain and disappointment in myself, I was literally caught up in listening to the praise song "Oh, How He Loves You and Me." For days I kept singing the words over and over in my mind until the reality of its truth penetrated my brokenness. Applying the principle of focusing on how much God loves me and forgives me eventually led to my being able to forgive myself. I forgave myself out of the experiential reality of my forgiveness that I had realized through the promises of Scripture and the lyrics of praise music.

LOCKED IN BY GUILT

When we cannot forgive ourselves, what we are really struggling with is an overwhelming sense of guilt over what we have done. Guilt is all too familiar an experience for all of us, yet it is counter to the whole concept of forgiveness. It is all too easy to "feel guilty." It is a feeling we probably have grown up with, so when we feel it, it's like an old familiar friend that has come to visit. We don't really want to push it away because it feels so normal.

Yet guilt is not actually a natural feeling. It must be learned. Technically speaking, guilt is a position in reference to the law. Either we are guilty of the crime or we are not guilty. It has nothing to do with whether or not we are *feeling* guilty. The feelings of guilt are something we have learned to experience over the years, and these feelings usually leave us in a paralyzed state.

If we are genuinely guilty, then we need to repent and make amends. If we are not guilty, then we need to reject the feelings of guilt and move on. There is nothing to be gained by staying in the position of "feeling guilty." That's one of the great things God's forgiveness has made possible—our freedom from guilt!

Forgiving Others/ Forgiving Ourselves

Forgiving ourselves is closely related to our forgiving others. If I am the offender, for instance, I need the offended party to be part of my own forgiving process, if possible. We may go through the process of forgiving ourselves to attempt to regain some sense of internal unity, but without our going to the person or persons we have offended and seeking to be reconciled with them, we leave the process unfinished.

Here, repentance and reconciliation are crucial, in part because we are in control of that part of the process. The offender can and must repent and make amends. Our healing comes within the context of the offended. If the offended refuses to participate in the process, we need someone else who will stand in the place of the offended one and hear our confessions.

Forgiving ourselves is also closely related to our ability to forgive others. P. A. Mauger and a group of colleagues did an interesting study on the relationship between forgiving oneself and forgiving others.[1] In their exploration of the general ability to forgive, they were seeking to examine and validate two assessment tools, one that measured the ability to forgive others and another that measured the ability to forgive oneself.

They found a direct correlation between the ability to forgive others and the ability to forgive oneself, even though these were clearly two separate concepts. They also found that these two abilities—especially the ability to forgive oneself—are related to some very important mental health issues. Those who are depressed or anxious are less likely to be able to forgive themselves, even though they may still be able to forgive others. Not surprisingly, they found that the worse our feelings about ourselves, the less likely we are to forgive ourselves. Just when we really need to forgive ourselves, we can't. But we must find a way because that is what God wants us to experience.

THE PROCESS OF FORGIVING MYSELF

The way we forgive ourselves is to walk down the same Path of Forgiveness we take when we forgive someone else. We need to fix appropriate blame—in this case, most likely on ourselves. But we need to admit it and say it out loud. Forgiveness is big enough to take care of that issue!

Then we must grieve. We can be angry with ourselves for our foolish behavior, and we need to experience sadness over the hurt that we have caused ourselves, and most likely, others.

As when we need to forgive others, it is good to share the process of forgiving ourselves with a trusted friend, someone who can keep us focused and moving down the path to forgiving.

After an appropriate time of grieving, we need to take the step of actually forgiving. Why not write oneself a letter of unconditional forgiveness? Then, in the presence of the trusted friend, we can burn the letter. Set markers that commemorate the forgiveness, so that you can never use your failure again to berate yourself.

One other point needs to be considered. When we have disappointed ourselves and need to forgive ourselves, we have probably hurt others as well. It is important that we can honestly take responsibility for what we have done and seek to make amends through repentance with those we have hurt. We can take the step toward reconciliation. If the other person is too hurt to listen, we must graciously back away, assuring him or her of our sincerity. And then wait for that person to be open to our needing to be forgiven. We cannot force someone to forgive us—it must flow freely from the other's heart. But we can create the *opportunity* for that person to forgive us according to his or her own timetable.

QUESTIONS TO CONSIDER

1. In what ways have you struggled with forgiving yourself?
2. What has made it hard for you to forgive yourself?
3. When you were able to forgive yourself, what made it possible?

CHAPTER EIGHT

A STEP BEYOND
FORGIVENESS

Yesterday you can't alter, but your reaction to yesterday you can.
The past you cannot change, but your response to your past you can.

MAX LUCADO

We've seen there are three paths we can choose when we are hurt. Two of them lead to destruction, and the third leads to forgiveness. The fruit of the Path of Denial and the Path of Bitterness will lead to destruction; the fruit of the Path of Forgiveness is freedom and new beginnings. But is there more we need to do beyond forgiving? Are there times we need to take an extra step beyond forgiveness?

David Augsburger tells a story about a scene he witnessed. He was at a dinner meeting where a United States senator was to give a speech to over 500 guests. Just as dinner was being finished, a waitress fumbled the plates of dessert and then dropped one on the shoulder of the senator. A wide smear of cake and lemon sauce spread down his coat, tie, and shirt, ending in his lap.

The senator scraped off what he could with a dinner knife while the humiliated waitress went to get some wet towels. She probably would have rather died, but she knew she had to help clean up the mess. As she helped him wipe off the remains of the dessert, the senator told her over and over it would be okay. But she was the picture of total embarrassment.

Just as the young waitress was ready to leave, the senator reached out "both hands to touch her still red face, drew her down, and gently kissed her cheek. The blush disappeared. A smile took its place. She left the room, radiant, head erect, alive."[1]

Augsburger then pointed out the meaning of the senator's action. He said the senator had taken a painful experience for this young woman—one that she would always remember with pain and humiliation—and had turned it into a story she would love to tell others. He had done what "a thousand words of 'I forgive you' could not do." He had taken a step beyond forgiveness.

WHEN A KISS CAN'T HAPPEN

Most of us aren't quick enough to think of doing on the spot what the senator did. How great it would be if we could. But what about the case where the one who offended us isn't interested in making any kind of amends, and the thought of taking a step beyond forgiveness is simply impossible. Or what if the hurt is so far in the past that we really can't think of anything more we can do to finish the task. And what do we do when the offending person is no longer in our lives? Is there something that needs to be done after we have gone through the process of forgiving? Sometimes.

There may be times when we have worked hard on the processing of our forgiving, and yet we still feel like there is something unfinished within us. Randy, a pastor friend of mine, told me of a particular Sunday morning when he came to the service in his church. Three different people stood out to him in the congregation that morning. These were three people who were a constant irritant to him as their pastor. They weren't a real big problem, just an ongoing frustration. He hadn't thought of them as someone he needed to forgive—he just tried to avoid them whenever he saw them.

As he went through the early parts of the service, it seemed God was making him intensely aware of these three people and his frustrations with them. He related that he had a conversation with God that went something like this:

God: You see those three people?
Randy: Yes, God.
God: You sure you see those three people?
Randy: Yes, but why are You showing them to me?
God: I think it's time you dealt with your feelings about
   them.
Randy: I don't feel that strongly about them. I forgive
   them whenever they irritate me.

God: You still feel strongly enough that I'm talking with
you about them right now.

Randy: What do You want me to do? I've got a sermon to
preach here pretty soon.

God: You can forget the sermon until you get My point.

Randy: But what's Your point?

God: Remember what My Son did.

Randy: I know. He forgave me my sins by His death on
the cross. You know I'm grateful for that, God.

God: That's not what I want you to see.

Randy: What am I missing?

God: What did My Son say as He was dying?

Randy went on to explain that while the service was going
on, he and God were having this ongoing conversation and
finally Randy got the point God wanted him to see. As he started to focus on Jesus' prayer from the cross, "Father, forgive them
for they don't know what they are doing," God seemed to be
impressing on him that He wanted Randy to pray that prayer for
those three people.

"As I did, a great peace came over me," Randy said to me. "It
was a major moment in my walk with the Lord." This was like a
step beyond forgiveness for Randy because he felt like he had
stayed current in his forgiving of each of these three people.
There was nothing that needed forgiveness now, for he sincerely
felt that the work of forgiving each of these people was current.
But God wanted him to take it a further step, and pray that He,
God, would forgive them as well.

But that wasn't the end of his story. He went on to tell me
what happened to Linda not too long after his conversation with
God. She was a young woman in his congregation who had a terrible relationship with her father. Her father was extremely cruel
to her while she was growing up and still was whenever she

allowed him to see her. He was very verbally abusive throughout her childhood, calling her all kinds of unprintable names for no reason. As she became a young woman, he didn't let up. Every time he was with her, he verbally abused her. Her confidence level as a woman was a zero—he had destroyed her on the inside. Even though she lived in the same town as he did, she had finally been able to limit any involvement with him.

Bothered by all this, in counseling, she began working on her issues regarding her father and the counselor wisely pointed her in the direction of forgiving her father. With the reassurance that forgiving him did not mean she had to have a relationship with him, she was finally able to forgive him. But something felt unfinished to her.

This didn't mean that she wanted to see her father, or to try to change her father. She knew he wasn't safe and so she had no desire to spend time with him. It just seemed unfinished. This led her to come in and talk with Randy, her pastor.

Randy shared with her the story of his conversation with God that Sunday morning—about his needing to pray that God forgive the offending persons, and then suggested that she consider praying that God would forgive her father, "for he didn't know what he was doing."

She dismissed his suggestion with the angry words, "He knew what he was doing!" and left his office. To her, it seemed unfair, unrealistic, and she was determined to forget about it. But God continued to work in her heart. Later she shared with Randy what had happened. For three days she had struggled with what he had suggested she do. Finally, at five o'clock in the evening on the third day, she gave up the struggle and prayed for her father, "Father, forgive him for he didn't know what he is doing." She immediately felt a release within, as if the forgiving process was finally complete. It had been a struggle, but now that she had prayed the prayer, she wasn't sure why, but somehow it felt settled. She went to bed later feeling a peace about her issues with her father.

The next morning, as she was getting ready to go to work, her doorbell rang. Wondering who could be at her home so early in the morning, she went and looked and saw her father outside. As she reluctantly opened the door, her father quickly walked into the living room. He seemed deeply agitated. He said, "I don't know what happened to me, but last night at dinner time, I was suddenly overwhelmed by the reality that I haven't treated you or your sisters like a father should and I need to get my life right." That's all he said, then he turned, walked out the door, and left. And Linda stood there for the longest time, simply amazed by what she had heard.

BINDING AND LOOSING

Something was set in motion by her prayer that was supernatural. It was almost as if God was set free in some way to begin to work in her father's life. This may be part of the meaning of Jesus' words to his disciples, "I tell you the truth, whatever you bind on earth will be bound in heaven, and whatever you loose on earth will be loosed in heaven" (Matt. 18:18, *NIV*). As she prayed for God to forgive him, she loosed something on Earth, and then it was then loosed in heaven! It seemed as if the Holy Spirit was now free to work in her father's life.

This statement by Jesus, recorded also in Matthew 16:19 after Peter's great declaration of who Jesus really is, has always been difficult to understand. Barclay suggests that when Jesus made this statement to Peter, he meant that "Peter would lay men's sins, bind them, to men's consciences, and then he would loose them from their sins by telling them of the divine love and the divine forgiveness of God."[2]

We will never in our lifetime fully
understand the interconnection between
what we do in our lives and the work of
the Holy Spirit in other people.

There are other interpretations, but this one seems to explain what might have happened when both Randy and Linda prayed that prayer. We could say that when we have a spirit of unforgiveness, we bind the sin on the one who has offended us as well as upon ourselves. There is certainly the sense that when we hold a grudge, we lock ourselves up to much of life, and we lock the other person up, at least in relation to ourselves.

And when we loose the sin, by our forgiving, we free ourselves. Perhaps the step beyond forgiving is to loose or set free the Holy Spirit to work in the life of the one who has hurt us. We will never in our lifetime fully understand the interconnection between what we do in our lives and the work of the Holy Spirit in other people. But this seems to be one of the ways to understand Jesus' statement about binding and loosing.

We see this principle of binding and loosing in two other biblical examples. These people prayed that God would forgive someone. In Acts 7:60, we see this prayer at work in Stephen as he is being stoned to death, which we mentioned earlier. He prayed, "Lord, don't charge them with this sin!" He was basically praying the same prayer as Jesus did on the cross—forgive them! He was loosing on Earth something that God would loose in heaven.

We also see this principle at work in the life of Job. After God has spent almost four chapters asking Job questions he couldn't answer, God turned to Eliphaz the Temanite and said, "I am angry with you and with your two friends, for you have not been right in what you said about me as my servant Job was. Now take seven young bulls and seven rams and go to my servant Job and offer a burnt offering for yourselves. My servant Job will pray for you, and I will accept his prayer on your behalf. I will not treat you as you deserve, for you have not been right in what you said about me, as my servant Job was" (Job 42:7,8).

God was angry with Job's three comforters. They had not

only offended God by speaking wrongly of him, but also they had tried to mislead Job with their false ideas. God chose not to deal with them by the standards they had just been lecturing about to Job. The interesting thing is that God didn't just forgive these three "comforters" by having them simply offer their sacrifices. Instead, God instructed them to have Job pray for them. Again, it seems that it was important for Job to "loose their sin on earth," so that they could be "loosed in heaven."

Perhaps Job prayed, "Father, forgive them, for they didn't understand what they were saying." We don't know what he prayed, but we do know that Eliphaz and his two friends were not free until Job had prayed for them. There is obviously incredible power released as we forgive and then take that step beyond forgiveness—when we pray that God will forgive the one who has sinned against us.

Obviously, not every situation that calls on us to forgive will call for that "extra step" beyond forgiving. But once we have forgiven, we may find it important to pray for those who "sin against us," and to ask that God will "forgive them, for they didn't know what they were doing."

QUESTIONS TO CONSIDER

1. Why do you think God wants us to "loose" someone by praying for God to forgive them?
2. What are some of the situations in your experience where this "step beyond" could apply?
3. If you believe that God is directing you to pray that God will forgive someone who has hurt you, what are some of the emotions you feel?

CHAPTER NINE

THE BENEFITS OF FORGIVENESS

On the day I forgave my father, my life began.

PAT CONROY

W e've looked at three paths open to us when we are faced with someone sinning against us. What we also need to understand is that our choosing the path of forgiveness is not only important for our spiritual growth, but it is also important to us in terms of our physical and emotional health.

PHYSICAL BENEFITS

A number of years ago I was talking about forgiveness on the Minirth-Meier Clinic radio program when an assistant quietly came into the room and handed us a piece of paper. She had been researching forgiveness on the Internet and had found a fascinating piece of information. I've never forgotten it, though I could never find it again, except when it was reported in the Minirth-Meier New Life Clinic newsletter in January 1995.

The assistant had given us the report of a study conducted by Duke University Medical School. It stated that the number one killer in the United States was not cancer, heart disease, AIDS or any of the other commonly cited causes of death. Instead of looking at disease, the researchers looked at attitudes and emotions and found the number-one killer was a spirit of unforgiveness.

The researchers were looking at what might be called the "hidden death syndrome" related to unforgiveness. They were saying that hidden behind heart disease, cancer, and the other fatal diseases in our country lies an emotional mind-set of unforgiveness.

What happens to our bodies when we don't forgive? We live in a state of stress, leading eventually to burnout, both physical and emotional. A simple example is what happens when we have an unresolved conflict with someone at church. We may not be consciously thinking about it, but as we get ready to go to church, tension and stress begin to build up within us. When we arrive, we are careful to park in a space that will be far from where the other person usually parks. We enter the church through a different door, and if we see the other person, we change our direction and avoid seeing him or her.

Who's running our life at that point? Certainly we aren't. Our behaviors are determined by our desire to avoid running into the other person. When we finally take our seat, we are ruminating about the offense we experienced at the hands of that other person and feel a smoldering sense of anger.

Whenever we feel lingering stress or tension, or struggle with long-term feelings of anger, various hormones are released into our bodies. One is adrenaline, significant blood levels of which can have serious consequences for the heart, nervous system and immune system when maintained long term. In the early stages, we may experience headaches, muscle tension, fatigue, problems with sleeping, digestive problems, ulcers and, of course, depression.

If we take the Path of Denial or the Path of Bitterness, and continue to experience elevated blood levels of adrenaline and other hormones associated with chronic anger, our blood pressure could become chronically elevated, we could develop heart disease or we could become more susceptible to cancer. Medical research no longer questions the connection between the attitudes of unforgiveness and chronic low-level anger, and major forms of illness; current research now places greater focus on the *degree* to which these attitudes contribute to these major illnesses.

One study of cancer patients who had been diagnosed as terminal (expected to live six months or less) found that those who completed a special anger-management program—along with traditional medical treatment—were more likely to go into remission than those who only received the traditional medical treatment. In that program, patients were taught different ways to handle their anger and were given specific training in how to move from an attitude of unforgiveness to an attitude of forgiveness.

Long-term follow-up of these patients revealed that many experienced remissions from the cancer for a number of years. When the cancer did return, researchers found that this relapse could be correlated with a return to old ways of handling anger and forgiveness. One doctor noted that forgiveness, as taught by Jesus, was the "2000-year-old health tip."

Type A behavior has been blamed for an increase in cardiovascular disease ever since it was identified as a lifestyle. More recent studies conducted by Redford Williams have found that Type A behavior alone isn't the cause, but high scores on a "hostility" scale were the predictive factor.[1] Hostility is a long-term anger that could easily be synonymous with bitterness. Type A people will, almost by nature, pick the Path of Bitterness, but when they are taught ways to reduce their hostility and practice a pattern of forgiving, they can become healthy Type A's.

A study of the effect of forgiveness on older adults found that the more these adults had been able to forgive offenses earlier in their lives, the better their physical health in old age. An interesting finding in this study was that the motivation for forgiving was also important. Simply to forgive for one's own benefit wasn't effective. One had to forgive for the sake of the offender, or because a person believed forgiveness was the right thing to do—an act of obedience. They had to "forgive from the heart," as Jesus instructed us.

There are apparently two ways that forgiveness benefits us physically. One way is through the reduction of stress. When we choose not to forgive, we end up with a "potent mixture of bitterness, anger, hostility, hatred, resentment,"[2] and the fear of having the same thing happen to us again. These negative emotions will increase our blood pressure and lead to hormonal changes that are linked to heart disease, the impairment of our immune system, and even to impaired neurological functions, including our memory. This always ultimately leads to some kind of health problem.

The second way forgiveness benefits us physically is that forgiving people have stronger social networks. And people who have strong friendships and strong familial networks are physically healthier. This is based in part on the research of Charlotte VanOyen Witvliet, from Hope College in Holland, Michigan, who said, forgiveness "should be incorporated into one's personality, a way of life, not merely a response to specific results."[3] Another writer regards forgiveness "as the tofu of the soul, a healthful alternative to the red meat of anger and vengeance."[4] He suggested that forgiving is an act that always benefits the forgiver.

EMOTIONAL BENEFITS

In an attempt to see what really helped people forgive, a group of researchers carefully designed a project where they could attempt to see if either of two specific variables really helped people become more forgiving.[5] One variable was *empathy*. To look at this factor, they attempted to measure how much the person could identify with the problems and frailties of the offender on an emotional level. The other variable was called *perspective-taking*. Here the measure was of how much the person could identify with the offender on the mental level.

They randomly set up three groups. One of the skills was taught in each of the first two groups. The first group went through a series of exercises that were designed to help people forgive by convincing them that revenge and withholding forgiveness were bad for them. The researchers put the second group through exercises that sought to generate empathy in the group member for the offender. The third group was a control;

that group performed neither kind of exercise. (They did go through the exercises after the project was completed.)

When results from the first two groups were compared with those of the control group, both methods were found to be effective in helping people forgive. But they also found that the ability to empathize with the offender—which also involved some degree of taking the perspective of the other person—was more directly related to a person's ability to forgive.

Empathy and perspective-taking are two skills found in emotionally mature people. Empathy is emotional understanding of the offender, while perspective-taking is cognitive, mental understanding. The better able we are to put ourselves in someone else's shoes, the better the quality of our relationships and our own mental health.

In helping people personalize the forgiving process with someone who has hurt them deeply, I often ask them to use their imagination to visualize themselves having a conversation with Jesus. In that mental conversation, they talk to Jesus about how much the other person has hurt them. After a short while, I then ask them to ask Jesus why that other person might have done such a thing to them. And then I let them quietly listen to the inner voice of Jesus helping them see the problem from the other person's perspective.

I remember our doing this with one of our own grown sons. He had hurt all of us deeply, and Jan and I were struggling with our feelings of anger and hurt. One time, as I was leading a group through the imagining exercise, Jan went through it as well and talked to Jesus about that son. And when she asked Jesus why that son had acted that way, what she heard was a description of that son's own fears, hurts and struggle with life. As she and I talked about it, we were both able to see some of the pain that our son was experiencing and were able to release our anger and forgive.

Much of what Peter Bliss has found in his work with the men at the Rescue Mission is that when these men are able to forgive the hurts of the past, they are freed to begin to experience the opportunities of life today. He has also developed a debt-canceling program for couples, and more recently he has been presenting this program to the whole church body. As I have done this debt-canceling with YWAM groups in different parts of the world, the results have been very similar. When people forgive a person for a major hurt, they are literally set free. The bondage of the past is broken.

We often believe we are retaining or regaining a sense of power and control when we withhold forgiveness, but that is a false sense of control. We think we are in control, but the truth is quite the opposite. When we forgive, we actually regain self-control when we give up control. This principle was demonstrated in a study of persons who had been deeply hurt by a divorce. The researcher found:

> For those people who forgave from the heart, their sense of personal power increased over time. They felt more in control of their personal decisions, finances, feelings, and responses to the offender. Those who did not forgive, or who forgave out of fear or out of a desire for personal gain, found that their sense of power *decreased* over time.[6]

Forgiveness restores the belief that we have some power over what happens in our own lives.

RELATIONAL BENEFITS

Perhaps one of the greatest benefits we can experience when we forgive is the possibility of a restored relationship. Forgiveness is an essential ingredient for a successful, satisfying marriage and happy, successful families. In families where forgiveness is taught by both word and example, negative outcomes are minimized. Forgiveness is the opposite of denial and family secrets, both of which contribute to increasing family problems. Genuine forgiveness never does away with accountability; accountability is a given. Yet genuine forgiveness with accountability in relationships always opens up the possibility of greater levels of trust and intimacy.

Reconciliation in relationships is only possible when there has been forgiveness. As we've noted, not every relationship can or should be restored, but when forgiving, we always want to consider the possibility of reconciliation. "Connectedness is preferable to individualism; human solidarity is our goal rather than isolation; open communication systems more healthful than closed and cut-off relationships. A concern for healing, a hope for restoration, and a commitment to reconnection biases"[7] everything we do as believers.

David expresses this in Psalm 133, where he says,

> How wonderful it is, how pleasant, when brothers live together in harmony! For harmony is as precious as the fragrant anointing oil that was poured over Aaron's head, that ran down his beard and onto the border of his robe. Harmony is as refreshing as the dew from Mount Hermon that falls on the mountains of Zion. And the Lord has pronounced his blessing, even life forevermore.

The apostle Paul urges us, "Do your part to live in peace with everyone, as much as possible" (Rom 12:18). Again, in 1 Thessalonians 5:13-15, he urges us,

> Remember to live peaceably with each other. Brothers and sisters, we urge you to warn those who are lazy.

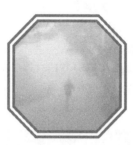

Genuine forgiveness never does
away with accountability.

Encourage those who are timid. Take tender care of
those who are weak. Be patient with everyone. See that
no one pays back evil for evil, but always try to do good
to each other and to everyone else.

Revenge, or getting even, is never part of our lifestyle—but
forgiveness is to always be there.

SPIRITUAL BENEFITS

We've already noted what happens when we harbor a spirit of
unforgiveness with someone at our church. Imagine what happens during worship. How can we be free to worship when we are
holding a grudge against a brother or a sister? We can't. That's
why Jesus instructs us,

So if you are standing before the altar in the Temple,
offering a sacrifice to God [or are standing in the church,
worshipping in song], and you suddenly remember that
someone has something against you, leave your sacrifice there beside the altar. Go and be reconciled to that
person. Then come and offer your sacrifice to God
(Matt. 5:23-24).

Notice that Jesus was referring to us as the offender. As the
offender, it is our duty to go and make things right. However, if
we are harboring a spirit of unforgiveness, we have become co-
offenders and need to confess our spirit of unforgiveness and
make amends. When we fail to do this, we begin to isolate ourselves, not only from other people, but also from our relationship
with God. Our prayers become empty, and we feel hypocritical.
The Scriptures are empty of meaning. Other believers irritate us.
We become cynical about our faith and about life.

When we give up our unforgiving spirit, we experience new freedom in our personal lives and new meaning in our spiritual lives. We don't feel as isolated. We are more at peace with our faith and beliefs. We feel like God is there, present in our lives, and we have a wider perspective on all of life that adds meaning to our own lives.

IN CONCLUSION

Forgiveness is getting a lot of good press these days in the secular setting. In counseling, secular therapists and researchers are looking at forgiveness as a powerful therapeutic tool that has very positive effects.

We need to be careful that we do not take forgiveness out of its spiritual context, however, because forgiveness can best be understood only in the context of our being forgiven by God. The theological and spiritual roots of forgiveness are what give it its healing power. Apart from that, forgiveness can be a helpful tool but never to the same degree as when it is connected to the reality of God's forgiveness of us.

God longs for us to be forgiving people. Counselors and pastors need to model forgiveness; families need to model forgiveness as a way of life; couples need to model forgiveness with each other in order to build strong marriages. We can only truly model forgiveness when we ourselves know how to forgive. When we can recognize our own sinfulness and see the universality of sin, we are less likely to develop a condemning spirit. Whenever we experience a deep wound in our souls through the action of another, we have a choice as to which path we are going to take. Make certain you pick the right path—the Path of Forgiveness!

When we led the seminar at the church in Michigan, I was asked to write the prayer of confession for the morning worship service. It is my prayer for myself and for you who have read this book:

Father God, we confess our wrongdoing to You, knowing that you graciously forgive. But some of our wrongdoing is not that obvious, even to ourselves.

We confess that many times we have an unforgiving spirit.
We seek in our hearts the revenge that belongs only to You.
We quietly nurse the hurt caused by sins that have been done to us.
We sometimes even enjoy the feelings of superiority that can come from being victimized by others.

We acknowledge these types of sins as well—the sins done to us—and how we so often sin in our response to these hurts.

But You graciously forgive all our sins, and we, with thanksgiving, accept Your forgiveness and pray that You will create within us a forgiving spirit. In the name of Your Son Jesus, who paid the price for our forgiveness.
Amen.

CHAPTER TEN

QUESTIONS OFTEN ASKED CONCERNING FORGIVENESS

As I travel and speak on forgiveness, it seems the same questions invariably come from the audience. Even though we have discussed most of these points earlier in the book, hearing the information in response to these questions may help reinforce the answers.

QUESTION 1:
Are There Situations When the Damage Done by an Offender Is So Severe That Forgiveness Is Inappropriate?

Although it may certainly feel that forgiveness is impossible when we begin to look at the deepest hurts inflicted upon us, it is important to understand that there is nothing that can happen in our lives that is beyond our ability to forgive. We must always put our ability to forgive in the context of how much we have been forgiven. That's one of the main points of Jesus' parable in Matthew 18 regarding the unforgiving servant. Here is a man who had been forgiven a debt he could never repay. It was his failure to internalize the reality of his forgiven-ness that kept him from forgiving his friend. Jesus is clearly saying that when we compare what we are called on to forgive—even the worst possible sin against us—it is less than what God in Christ has forgiven us. It is out of our gratitude for His forgiveness that we can always forgive.

It is important to remember that the deeper the hurt and the earlier the hurt takes place in our lives, the more time we need to work through the process of forgiving. We are always called on to forgive, but the time frame for that forgiveness will vary with the severity of the offense.

QUESTION 2:
What If the One Who Has Hurt Me Is Seeking My Forgiveness, and I'm Not Yet Ready to Forgive?

This is where our understanding of the three stages of forgiving helps us. It begins with the decision that we are going to forgive; followed by the process of forgiving which includes grieving what was lost; and finally, the third stage where we finalize the forgiveness. When someone realizes quickly their offense, and they are seeking our forgiveness while we are still in the early stage, reacting to the hurt, we can very simply say something like, "Yes, I'm going to forgive you, but I'm not quite ready yet. I need to work through some of my feelings first." An example would be if someone seriously hurt you physically and then realized what they had done and quickly apologized. At that point, you are probably not ready to listen to their apology—you want to get some medical attention first, and then deal with the apology. In the same way, when the offense cuts deeply into our emotions, we need some time to heal before we are ready to work on the forgiving.

At the same time, there needs to be some limits to the time frame for our working through the pain. Grieving takes time, but there is an ending to it. This is when we need some trustful companions on the journey with us who can keep us accountable to get to the forgiving.

QUESTION 3:
What If My Working Through the Forgiving Process Means I Might Possibly Reveal Some Family Secrets That Cause Hurt to Others?

This is an important question that often comes up. Sometimes when we have been abused in our family, we want at some point to confront the abuser. That possible confrontation could bring family secrets out into the open. Or maybe we have been the offender in some secret way, like an affair, and in the forgiving of ourselves, we feel the need to confess what has been secret up to this point.

We need to understand our motives. Sometimes our desire to confront is a hidden desire for revenge of sort. Or our need to confess is really our need to transfer our guilty feelings, or rid ourselves of them. In either case, we need to consider what the effect might be of our bringing the secret out into the open.

On the other hand, families are as sick as their secrets. And family health often requires that we bring the secret out of the darkness into the light. One woman shared with me at a conference that she had several years before had a brief affair. She had confessed her sin with the Lord, but her husband had never known of the affair. She wanted to confess to him what she had done. I agreed with her need to confess but suggested she wait, and while waiting, that she pray for a very clear, specific, God-given opportunity for her to confess.

Some months later she wrote me and thanked me for what I had suggested. She said she had prayed, and some months later, God gave her the perfect opportunity to confess. Her husband was able to hear her heart and forgive her, and they both experienced great healing in their marriage.

One of the reasons for waiting to consider reconciliation until after we have forgiven is that once we have forgiven, our expectations are greatly reduced. It also gives us time to heal, so we can more accurately understand both our own motives as well as to listen to God for the right timing for bringing the secret into the light.

QUESTION 4:
It Doesn't Seem Fair That I Am the One Hurt, and I Am Also the One Who Has to Do the Work of Forgiving. The Offending Person Seems to Get Off Too Easily.

It isn't fair! But remember, the one who benefits from forgiving is the one who does the forgiving. Our forgiving the offender does not in any way benefit the offender. One can easily say that forgiving is a very "selfish" act—or maybe a better word would be "selfcarish." It is selfish in that it focuses on us, but it is also a caring act, in that we are the ones who are set free. We are the ones who benefit physically, emotionally and spiritually.

Lewis Smedes says, "forgiving is the *only* way we have to a better fairness in our unfair world; it is love's unexpected revolution against unfair pain and it alone offers strong hope for healing the hurts we so unfairly feel."[1] We don't revise the past; we accept it.

QUESTION 5:
How Can I Know the Offender Is Sincere When He or She Asks for Forgiveness?

Of course, this assumes the offender is seeking forgiveness, which as we have noted does not always happen. But when the offender does come to us and ask for forgiveness, only the offended one can determine the sincerity of the apology. This may be difficult because usually the offense causes us to lose trust in the person. Trust is only rebuilt over time and is restored as we see consistency in the other person and an openness to whatever it takes to rebuild the relationship. It takes a seeking on the part of the offender to show us genuine sorrow over what happened. We need to listen to our own hearts as well, for many times we need also to learn to trust our own instincts again as we listen to the efforts of the offender to make amends.

But the problem is always compounded by the fact that we can never know for certain the motivation of another person. We can only observe their sincerity over time. However, if you are working with a counselor in the process, it may be helpful to have an objective outsider who can help you evaluate the sincerity of the one apologizing. You may even ask the offender to come with you to a session in order to apologize in front of the counselor, who can give you their "read" on the sincerity of the apology. You would probably only do this with a counselor when the relationship is important and the offender is willing.

QUESTION 6:

What Do I Do If I Still Don't Want to Forgive?

When we are still reluctant to forgive, we need to ask ourselves several questions. First, Are you trying to protect yourself from further hurt by your refusal to forgive? Are you trying to forgive something that is ongoing, and do you need to set some healthy boundaries first? Do you feel empowered by your not forgiving? In other words, you need to examine what you are holding on to—besides the offense—that is blocking out your ability to move into forgiveness.

The other thing you should do at this point is to spend some time understanding how God has forgiven you. Remembering that when you were God's enemy, and were very unlovely, God loved you so much he forgave you through Christ's death on the cross. Read over Romans 5:1-11 and Matthew 18:21-35. Pray honestly: Tell God you don't want to forgive even though you know it is what he wants from you. Ask him to help you want to forgive.

QUESTION 7:
How Do I Forgive When I Have to Keep Seeing the Offending Person?

It is hard to forgive when the person who has hurt you keeps showing up in your life. Their presence is a continual reminder of the hurt. For this reason, you may need to set some temporary limits in being around that person, even if it is family. Note that it is a temporary separation that allows you some time to heal. You may say to the other person something like, "I need some time alone for a while. I'll get in touch with you later."

Of course, if it is your spouse, you can't avoid seeing him or her. In that situation, the forgiving process needs to be openly discussed. And your partner needs to give you the time you need to experience healing. Their seeking a "too quick" forgiveness doesn't help the healing process.

Some Final Thoughts

What I have described in this book may seem like a simple, clear process that proceeds smoothly once you embark on the journey. It usually isn't that simple. But don't let that stop you from the task. Whenever you heal the hurt you didn't deserve, you are experiencing an act of obedience that represents a new beginning. Sometimes, the miraculous happens, and God seems to step into the process in ways you could never have imagined. Other times, we must plod along, seemingly on our own as we move towards forgiving. But even in those times, the miracle of forgiving is taking place. God always honors the move toward forgiveness—it is His plan for us. When we forgive we are giving God the opportunity to work miracles in our lives in His way and in His time.

ENDNOTES

Chapter One
1. Pat Conroy, *The Prince of Tides* (New York: Bantam Dell Publishing Group, 1987).
2. Joyce Hollyday, "Hearts of Stone," *Sojourners Magazine* (March–April 1998).
3. Quoted in David Augsburger, *The Freedom of Forgiveness* (Chicago: Moody, 1970, 1988), p. 15.
4. Ibid., p. 46.
5. *Webster's College Dictionary*, s.v. "forgiveness."

Chapter Three
1. "An Unnatural Act," *Christianity Today* (April 8, 1991), p. 36.

Chapter Four
1. Becky Burkert, *Holland Sentinel*, May 16, 1999, sec. E, p.1.
2. Simon Wiesenthal, *The Sunflower* (New York: Schoken, 1998), p. 42.
3. Ibid., pp. 53-54.
4. Ibid.
5. Ibid., p. 98.
6. Ibid., p. 220.
7. Ibid., p. 121.
8. *When Forgiveness Seems Impossible* (Grand Rapids, Mich.: RBC Ministries, 1994).
9. Ibid.
10. Wiesenthal, *The Sunflower*, p. 211.

Chapter Five
1. Virgil Elizondo, "I Forgive but I Do Not Forget," in Casiano Floristan and Christian Duquoc, *Forgiveness* (Edinburgh: T & T Clark, 1986).

Chapter Seven
1. P. A. Mauger et al., "The Measurement of Forgiveness: Preliminary Research," *Journal of Psychology and Christianity* 11 (1992): 170–80.

Chapter Eight
1. David Augsburger, *The Freedom of Forgiveness* (Chicago: Moody, 1970, 1988), pp. 107-108.

2. William Barclay, *The Gospel of Matthew, Volume Two* (Edinburgh: The Saint Andrew Press, 1957), p. 160.

Chapter Nine

1. Redford Williams and Virginia Williams, *Anger Kills* (New York: Random House, l993).
2. Jordana Lewis and Jerry Adler, "Forgive and Let Live," *Newsweek* (September 27, 2004), p. 52.
3. Ibid.
4. Ibid.
5. Michael E. McCullough, Steven J. Sandage, and Everett L. Worthington, Jr., *To Forgive Is Human* (Downers Grove, IL: InterVarsity Press, l997), p. 192.
6. Ibid., p. 201.
7. David Augsburger, *The Freedom of Forgiveness* (Chicago: Moody, 1970, 1988), p. 147.

Chapter Ten

1. Lewis Smedes, *Forgive and Forget* (San Francisco: Harper and Row, 1984), p. 124.

More of the Best from Dr. David Stoop

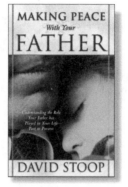